The Idea of a
Christian College

Other Books by Todd C. Ream and Perry L. Glanzer

Christian Faith and Scholarship:
An Exploration of Contemporary Debates

Christianity and Moral Identity in Higher Education

Other Books by Todd C. Ream

A Parent's Guide to the Christian College:
Supporting Your Child's Mind and Spirit During the College Years
(with Timothy W. Herrmann & C. Skip Trudeau)

Other Books by Perry L. Glanzer

The Quest For Russia's Soul:
Evangelicals and Moral Education in Post-Communist Russia

The Idea of a
Christian College

A Reexamination for Today's University

TODD C. REAM
AND
PERRY L. GLANZER

CASCADE *Books* · Eugene, Oregon

THE IDEA OF A CHRISTIAN COLLEGE
A Reexamination for Today's University

Cascade Books
An Imprint of Wipf and Stock Publishers
199 W. 8th Ave., Suite 3
Eugene, OR 97401

www.wipfandstock.com

ISBN 13: 978-1-61097-327-4

Cataloguing-in-Publication data:

Ream, Todd C.

The idea of a Christian college : a reexamination for today's university / Todd C. Ream and Perry L. Glanzer.

xvi + 158 pp. ; 23 cm. Includes bibliographical references.

ISBN 13: 978-1-61097-327-4

1. Church and college. I. Glanzer, Perry L. II. Title

CALL NUMBER 2013

Manufactured in the U.S.A.

The cover photo is of the Baylor Sciences Building on the campus of Baylor University in Waco, Texas, was taken by Matt Pagant, and is used with his permission.

For teachers such as Arthur F. Holmes who made a difference:
Steven Benke, W. Winfred Moore, Dennis M. Campbell,
M. Lee Upcraft, and Joseph Robert Weaver.
The challenge and the support you provided me forged a debt I can only
hope to repay through the service I provide my own students
—Todd C. Ream

For my parents:
Joseph and Cynthia Glanzer
the best Christian educators I know
—Perry L. Glanzer

Hearing that Jesus had silenced the Sadducees, the Pharisees got together. One of them, an expert in the law, tested him with this question: "Teacher, which is the greatest commandment in the Law?"

Jesus replied: "'Love the Lord your God with all your heart and with all your soul and with all your mind.' This is the first and greatest commandment. And the second is like it: 'Love your neighbor as yourself.' All the Law and the Prophets hang on these two commandments."

—MATTHEW 22:34–40

Contents

Acknowledgments

ONE OF THE BLESSINGS that comes with writing a book is realizing just how many people to whom you owe some debt of gratitude. No set of ideas emerges from absolute isolation. Afforded by the grace of God, human beings are given the opportunity to live in and to appreciate the wisdom we are able to share with one another. Despite our depravity, our best moments grant glimpses of the social nature of the triune God we worship.

We must first begin by thanking the communities of faith in which we find our souls nourished—Jerome Christian Church in Greentown, Indiana and First Baptist Church in Woodway, Texas. In these places we hear the Word and gather around the Lord's table with fellow believers who remind us that the work we do in Christian universities matters, if for no other reason than many of them entrust the education of their sons and daughters to us. We hope that what is in these pages reflects the highest ideals of that trust.

The university communities where we serve have also proven to be generous sources of support and encouragement. At Taylor University, Tim Herrmann and Skip Trudeau offered their friendship as well as constant reminders of what the ideals we are striving to communicate in this book look like in person. At Indiana Wesleyan University, David Wright, Jerry Pattengale, and Alleta Tippey not only labored to provide funds to support this project but they also offered their friendship. At Baylor University, the whole university provided rich contexts for conversations about the most critical concerns facing the Christian university. In particular, colleagues within the department such as Nathan Alleman, Laine Scales, and Rishi Sriram, as well as those outside the department such as Thomas Kidd and Wes Null, proved to be critical to the success of this project.

Several friends and colleagues across the country took the time to read through our manuscript, challenge our assumptions, and think about how what we are arguing would be received by the audience we have in mind. We cannot say thank you enough to the input given by graduate students in the Master of Arts in Higher Education Program at Taylor University (Lisa Barber, Emily Bryan, Isaac Bryan, Julie Caldwell, David Chizum, Julie Cline, Janette DeLozier, Logan Denney, Cody Lloyd, Joo Yong Park, David Restrick, Erin Slater, Jeff Strietzel, Eric Strong, Heather Tyner, Lance Vanderberg, Katie Westrate, Megan Wilhelmson, and Amy Wilson) and undergraduate students in the John Wesley Honors College at Indiana Wesleyan University (Ashely DeMichael, Lauren Martin, Olivia Ortmann, and Jason Stanley). In addition, friends such as Brian C. Clark and Elmer John Thiessen made valuable contributions that greatly enhanced the quality of the argument we are striving to offer.

Of course, our families provide forms of support and love that defy measure. Our children, Addison Danielle Ream, Ashley Caitlin Ream, Bennett Glanzer, and Cody Glanzer, offer respites of laughter and the kinds of probing questions only children can ask. Part of the reason we labor in the manner we do is because we want to ensure we have committed whatever talents God has given us to a form of education from which they and all children can benefit.

Our wives, Sara C. Ream and Rhonda Glanzer, are the clearest forms of God's grace in this world we can appreciate. Their love draws out convictions and abilities from within us that we otherwise did not know existed. We are not certain who we would have become without them and thus we thank God every day for bringing them into our lives.

From Todd—As a person who now embraces the noble calling of teaching, I am privileged to dedicate this book to teachers who influenced me: Steve Benke (Whittier Christian High School), W. Winfred Moore (Baylor University), Dennis M. Campbell (Duke University), M. Lee Upcraft (Penn State University), and Joseph Robert Weaver (Oklahoma Baptist University). They were generous with their time, long on patience, willing to correct, and, like all great teachers, graciously extended hope. My parents, Charles and Linda Ream, were of course the first great teachers in my life. I was fortunate, however, to appropriately dedicate my previous book (with Timothy W. Herrmann and C. Skip Trudeau) *A Parent's Guide to the Christian College*, to them. As a result, I am now in the position of also starting to repay the debt I owe to these other great teachers who influenced my life.

From Perry—I want to dedicate this book to the greatest Christian educators in my life: my parents. Their teaching, modeling, and love grounded me in a Christian identity and love for God that sustained me through an almost completely secular education that, while full of wonderful teachers, depth, and challenge, rarely pointed to Christ as Lord. Fortunately, they always did.

Anything good that can be found within certainly bears the influence of the individuals to whom we dedicate this book. Of course, they are not to blame for any deficiencies these pages harbor.

Todd C. Ream and Perry L. Glanzer
Greentown, Indiana and Hewitt, Texas
Advent 2013

Preface

O<small>N</small> O<small>CTOBER</small> 8, 2011, Christian higher education and the church lost a voice that will fortunately reverberate for generations through the lives of individuals privileged enough to encounter it. Arthur F. Holmes taught philosophy at Wheaton College for almost four and a half decades. Countless Wheaton students heard his voice directly while even larger numbers of people encountered his touching words through his writings. Upon hearing the news of Holmes's death, C. Steven Evans, a former student of Holmes and now a philosophy professor at Baylor University, contributed a piece to *Books and Culture* entitled "Arthur Holmes: A Life Well-Lived." While many components of Holmes's life made it well-lived, Evans was quick to note, "Above all, Art was a great teacher."[1]

In 1975, Holmes published the book for which he would likely become best known—*The Idea of a Christian College*. At the time, Holmes could not have guessed his book would be in print thirty plus years later and would have enlisted such a large following. This work's thoughtful yet accessible style made it a long-standing choice for reading lists on Christian college campuses across the country and around the world. Countless numbers of first-year students read and discussed this book as part of their introduction to the Christian college experience. Some faculty members still require this book in settings populated by these students such as orientation groups and first-year seminars.

In 1987, a revised edition of the book was offered as a way of introducing some needed material—chapters concerning the relationship the liberal arts share with career preparation and the marks or definitive qualities of an educated person. Otherwise, the version published thirty-five years ago

---

1. C. Steven Evans, "Arthur Holmes: A Life Well-Lived," *Books and Culture* (January-February 2012) 5.

remains unchanged. The insights Holmes initially offered are still received by an appreciative and eager audience. However, enough has changed in the church, the academy, and the culture at large to necessitate a full-scale reexamination of the ideas in this critical book.

What we intend to undertake in the following pages is a reexamination of the idea of the Christian college in the light of these changes, particularly recent scholarly contributions within Christian higher education that have transformed discussions currently taking place. In this respect, our effort seeks to do what Jaroslav Pelikan's *The Idea of a University: A Reexamination* did in relation to John Henry Newman's *The Idea of a University*. In order to do so, we would like to focus on three particular contributions and changes—the increasing importance placed upon the role of worship and the church, the rise of scholarly attention to the central question, "What does it mean to be fully human?," and the transformation of many Christian colleges into Christian universities.

First, the new ecclesiastical emphasis has focused upon worship's rightful place in orienting our lives. Through teaching us to worship, the church orients our loves in ways that then help us to interpret and live the rest of our lives. As Stanley Hauerwas mentions in his memoir *Hannah's Child* (and as is discussed at greater length in chapter 1 of this book) the church teaches us that our lives depend "on learning to worship God."[2] Everything else we do as Christians is an extension of our willingness to learn such lessons in arenas such as the curricular (the formal course work) and the cocurricular (the activities and experiences outside the classroom). What would the idea for a Christian college look like if it was an extension of these lessons?

Second, Christian scholars have increasingly recognized our need to dethrone the impulse to reduce human beings to mere thinking selves or to selves divorced from our God-given identities. The church is more than just a place where cognitive debates over doctrine occur or a place where we talk about being a Christian separate from our other identities. The church, as an expression of the kingdom of God, exemplifies what it means for God to lay claim over all domains of our existence—our minds, our bodies, and our emotions, as well as what it means in specific divine and social relationships (to use our specific example, it involves learning what it means

2. Stanley Hauerwas, *Hannah's Child: A Theologian's Memoir* (Grand Rapids: Eerdmans, 2010) 159.

to be a good Christian, husband, American, son, man, neighbor, brother, professor, uncle, etc.).

In reality, learning to worship God makes demands upon what it means for us to be human in the largest and most all-encompassing terms possible. In *What is a Person?*, Christian Smith contends that few of us would find theories of personhood in the social sciences to be reflective of "what we understand about ourselves as people. Something about them fails to capture our deep subjective experience as persons, crucial dimensions of the richness of our own lives, what thinkers in previous ages might have called our 'hearts' and 'souls.'"[3] What would the idea for a Christian college look like if it reflected an understanding of human personhood that considers every dimension of our personhood?

Finally, since 1975, Christian colleges have changed in many ways. While some schools still resemble the liberal arts colleges Holmes had in mind, the majority of institutions that make up Christian higher education have undergone radical changes. On one level, they heeded Holmes's advice and enhanced the level of scholarly engagement pursued by their faculty and their students. On another level, they experienced unprecedented growth by almost any measure—students, faculty, administrators, facilities, budgets, and endowment dollars just to name a few.

For example, in a report entitled "The Booming Decade: CCCU Enrollment Trends for the 1990s," the Council for Christian Colleges and Universities (CCCU) noted that the number of students attending their member institutions grew 36.9 percent. In comparison, the number of students enrolled at all private colleges and universities grew 13.4 percent while the number of students enrolled in all higher education institutions in the United States grew 5.3 percent.[4] A host of Christian institutions of higher education eventually changed their name from "college" to "university" as an acknowledgment of the new organizational realities present on their campuses and today, 82 of the 119 (or 69 percent) CCCU institutions now call themselves universities.

For Holmes, the Christian college was "primarily an undergraduate teaching institution, not primarily a graduate school, nor a collection of professional schools, nor a research and public service institution as the

3. Christian Smith, *What Is a Person?* (Chicago: University of Chicago Press, 2010) 2–3.

4. Council for Christian Colleges and Universities, "The Booming Decade: CCCU Enrollment Trends for the 1990s," http://www.cccu.org/filefolder/Enrollment_Trends_Handout.doc (accessed May 9, 2012).

modern university has become. Its task is far more specific."[5] However, even some schools that still bear the name "college" (such as Arthur Holmes's Wheaton) now offer a host of graduate degrees and, in some cases, a handful of doctoral degrees. What would the idea for a Christian college look like if it reflected these organizational changes?

What follows in these pages is thus a reflection upon the significance of these considerable changes as well as other broad cultural shifts as a whole. We hope it proves to be a worthwhile investment of your time as you ponder the unique challenges and opportunities facing what we now refer to as "the Christian university." For the sake of reading ease, we have chosen to write in first person singular (with the exception of the introduction). Some of the stories reflect Todd's experiences. Some reflect Perry's. However, we take shared ownership over what you will read and hope it proves a charitable reexamination of the legacy established by *The Idea of a Christian College*. In the end, may we all summon comparable levels of clarity, passion, and prayerful discernment as Arthur Holmes did concerning the unique nature of institutions of higher learning called to bear the name "Christian."

5. Arthur F. Holmes, *The Idea of a Christian College* (Grand Rapids: Eerdmans, 1987) 7–8.

Introduction

Why a Christian University?

But by and large we have not dreamed large enough dreams.[1]
—Arthur F. Holmes, *The Idea of a Christian College*

"Calvin and Hobbes" offer some profound insights into higher education. And yes, we are talking about the old newspaper cartoon characters and not the famous theologian and philosopher. In one cartoon, while seated at a desk with paper and pen in hand, six-year-old Calvin explains to his imaginary stuffed-tiger friend, Hobbes, "I used to hate writing assignments, but now I enjoy them." Hobbes looks up, puzzled. Calvin continues, "I realized that the purpose of writing is to inflate weak ideas, obscure poor reasoning and inhibit clarity. With a little practice writing can be an intimidating and impenetrable fog!" He offers his paper to Hobbes, "Want to see my book report?" Hobbes dutifully reads the title, "The Dynamics of Interbeing and Monological Imperatives in Dick and Jane: A Study in Psychic and Transrelational Gender Modes." Calvin closes, "Academia here I come!"[2]

Unfortunately, academia and academics generate a reputation for complicating things to the point of confusion. Christian higher education should be different. Its mission should be simple, and the complexity

---

1. Arthur Holmes, *The Idea of a Christian College*, rev. ed. (Grand Rapids: Eerdmans, 1987) 11.

2. Bill Watterson, *The Complete Calvin and Hobbes*. Vol. 3 (Kansas City: Andrews McMeel, 2005) 140.

it provides should yield clarity. At one level, looking through the mission statements of the hundreds of secular and Christian universities in America, one will find one type of clarity. All of the institutions use verbs that denote their fundamental activity. They seek to "educate," "develop," "nurture," "transform," "provide," "prepare," "fashion," "cultivate," and more. In some way and through some kind of method, they hope to change students.

The most important question, however, is in what way do they hope to change those students. Change, transformation, and fashioning are not goods in and of themselves. What end do they seek or what goal do they have in mind? A recent book by Columbia University's Andrew Delbanco, *College: What It Was, Is, and Should Be* summarizes the three most common ends of colleges. First, some argue that colleges should prepare students to get jobs to help the national economy. Second, others claim higher education should develop leaders to further democracy, particularly America's form of liberal democracy. Third, others suggest that universities should contribute to the student's lifelong pursuit of happiness.[3] One usually finds some evidence of these three purposes in secular mission statements.

Yet, one finds something lacking in these three aims. They appear rather narrow. In his book *The End of Education*, former New York University professor and cultural critic Neil Postman claims that inspiring educational ends are supplied by a grand narrative that "tells of origins and envisions a future, a story that constructs ideals, prescribes rules of conduct, provides a source of authority, and, above all, gives a sense of continuity and purpose."[4] In other words, the story guiding education should answer a number of fundamental questions about existence, history, knowledge, truth, meaning, and the good life that then informs an educational institution's purpose.

The fact that Christian universities are guided by such a grand narrative means the purposes of Christian universities will diverge significantly from secular institutions. First, one often finds in the mission statements references to the extent of the education or formation envisioned. They talk about forming whole persons—the physical, rational, spiritual, and emotional aspects of the self. Second, one finds references to God, Christ, wisdom, and love that do not exist in secular statements. In general, these Christian mission statements reflect what Jesus revealed are the two most

---

3. Andrew Delbanco, *College: What It Was, Is and Should Be* (Princeton, NJ: Princeton University Press, 2012).

4. Neil Postman, *The End of Education* (New York: Vintage, 1995) 5–6.

important commands: "Love the Lord your God with all your heart and with all your soul and with all your mind and with all your strength" and "Love your neighbor as yourself" (Mark 12:29–31). The most important endeavor of institutions of higher education, Christian universities believe, should be cultivating, directing, ordering, and enriching our loves in the context of our most important relationships and human practices.

Christian universities exist because we need help with this endeavor, particularly as life becomes more complicated. Even when we achieve excellence in a narrow field, we need help in learning to love more as God first loved us. Consider the world's greatest athletes. All of them still have coaches. No matter if they are the greatest player in the world in golf, tennis, baseball, basketball, or any other sport—they still need a coach. The same proves true with almost any other endeavor. Talent and practice on their own are not enough. Loving God and others proves the same. Like any practice or endeavor in life, we need God's grace and human mentors to help us figure out how to do those things in particular contexts of life. While the goals of loving God and others are quite simple to articulate, we also need to recognize that love often becomes complicated when put into practice.

Moreover, Christians need to figure out how to engage in this multi-faceted love in a host of areas of our lives. One of us once asked the father of the champion of the National Junior Track and Field decathlon how his son trained for so many events. The father described how he sought coaches out for each different event to teach to his son the unique skills associated with each practice. Like a decathlete, students need to learn how to love God in multiple contexts and ways, and they need multiple mentors who can teach them how to do it. How can they love God as teachers, philosophers, engineers, historians, or accountants? How can they love God as citizens, spouses, sons or daughters, neighbors, brothers or sisters, men or women, stewards of creation, and more? How can they love God in these areas with all their heart, soul, mind, and strength? Going to a Christian university involves being around faculty, administrators, staff members, and other students who seek to guide them in this endeavor. Teaching at a Christian university involves a holistic commitment to mentor students in this manner.

Furthermore, this task becomes even more complicated as we move beyond our individual lives and form organizations and institutions to accomplish any number of tasks. How should the church care for the poor? How should schools best educate a diverse population? How can family members better love one another? How should a Christian hospital care for its patients and staff? If we are to provide an education that addresses these issues, it becomes clear that, as Arthur Holmes said, Christian higher education has "a constructive task, far more than a defensive one."[5] The purpose of this book is to construct the outlines of a vision for the Christian university that extends beyond limited Christian and secular visions of the university and the older visions of the Christian college that do not encompass the contemporary university.

LIMITED CHRISTIAN UNDERSTANDINGS OF THE UNIVERSITY

This simple yet complex conception of the purpose of a Christian university helps avoid a number of limited understandings about what higher education entails. One such conception involves the view that Christian higher education should focus primarily upon loving God with one's mind. This approach can take a variety of forms. On one end, Christian higher education may be seen primarily as a place that equips students with apologetics to defend the faith. While talking to a well-established Christian doctor at a local teaching hospital, one of our graduate students mentioned that he attended a Christian university. The doctor mentioned, "I bet you learn a lot of Christian apologetics there." While learning how to be "prepared to give an answer to everyone who asks you to give the reason for that hope that you have" (1 Pet 3:15) remains a responsibility of the Christian, the church, and the university, it does not fully capture the breadth of what should happen at a Christian university.

More broad-minded writers claim the role of the Christian university is to help students acquire a Christian worldview. While this understanding is more expansive than the last one and identifies the key role of enhancing cognitive abilities as the focus of Christian education, we need to recognize that it still narrows the focus of the Christian university. The end goal of the Christian university is not merely to educate students to think in theological terms, although that certainly is part of its job. In more complete terms, it involves teaching students how to love God with their whole being (their heart, soul, mind, and strength) and to do so in multiple contexts (as a student, neighbor, professional, citizen, possible parent, possible spouse, etc.). While helping students acquire a Christian worldview is an essential part of this larger goal, it focuses solely upon the cognitive part.

---

5. Holmes, *The Idea of a Christian College*, 7.

A second problematic understanding of a Christian university focuses primarily upon the moral dimension of life—it's a form of loving God with one's strength or one's behavior. This approach can take many shapes. A campus may be preoccupied with asking students to follow rules in the name of holiness or it can focus upon encouraging Christian practices. It can even tout service-learning or a particular commitment to justice. While all of these efforts are necessary and important (yes, even the campus rules) an inordinate focus on moral behavior or action can fail to capture the other elements of what a Christian education involves. Christian education that inordinately focuses upon outward forms of moral behavior fails to cultivate one's multifaceted love for God.

For example, let's consider campus rules. A Christian university that enforces basic rules about not cheating on tests or avoiding sexual immorality is merely enforcing the baseline standards for engaging in certain kinds of practices. Engagement in any meaningful practice requires such rules and enforcement. You cannot continue to double dribble in basketball, you cannot cheat if you seek to be an excellent scholar, and fidelity in one's sexual life is a basic practice regarding a marital relationship. Yet, faculty, administrators, and/or institutions that focus inordinately on rules and rule enforcement may lead students to miss cultivating a larger vision for excellence involved in a particular practice of life. While in the game of life, rules are important (particularly if you are not following them) merely knowing and following the rules does not make one a good or flourishing human being. One does not become a good basketball player by simply obeying the rules; one does not become an excellent scholar by not cheating; and while fidelity in marriage is critical, it does not ensure a marriage will flourish.

To guarantee their institution does not place an inordinate emphasis upon enforcing behavioral standards or simply focus on developing a Christian worldview, some Christians elevate the importance of loving God with one's heart. Numerous biblical passages would attest to this claim. As the Psalmist declares, "You do not delight in sacrifice, or I would bring it; you do not take pleasure in burnt offerings. The sacrifices of God are a broken spirit; a broken and contrite heart, O God, you will not despise" (Ps 51:16–17). Again, think about athletes who attained levels of excellence in their field. Without a passion for their particular practice, they could not train their mind and body.

Yet, we must also be careful about focusing only upon loving God with one's heart or one's affections to the exclusion of the other loves.

Sometimes our behaviors shape our heart, as Jesus reminds us when he says, "For where your treasure is, there will your heart be also" (Matt 6:21). Furthermore, numerous Christians throughout the ages have performed horrible deeds with the right heart because they lacked the intellectual insight or behavioral training to perform at levels of excellence. A good-hearted surgeon without rigorous mental education and the proper training of his or her hands can destroy patients' lives. Good-hearted charity can destroy the dignity of the poor, reinforce dependency, or distract one from deeper needs.[6] Furthermore, while we sometimes celebrate people with heart (e.g., underdog sports movies such as *Rocky*, *Hoosiers*, and *Rudy* to name only three) we need to recognize that having a heart for something does not necessarily mean one will achieve excellence in that particular field. Sometimes one needs certain gifts, natural or spiritual, and certainly one needs the necessary cognitive capacities and skills to achieve excellence. A Christian university must be committed to developing our love for God and God's creation in ways that capture our whole being.

LIMITED SECULAR CONCEPTIONS OF THE UNIVERSITY

The limitations of a secular university also become clear when both our life purpose and the purpose of higher education are conceived of in the comprehensive way described earlier. An example of the narrow nature of secular visions can be found in the famous philosopher Bertrand Russell's claim that education has two purposes: "to form the mind" and "to train the citizen."[7] Forming the mind is much narrower than forming a student's heart, soul, mind, and strength. Also, without any foundational reference point for this formation, it fails to identify how exactly the mind should be formed. In addition, creating citizens is an extremely narrow goal considering the full range of identities associated with what it means to be human. We are much more than citizens. We are or will become friends, professionals, neighbors, children, spouses, church members, men/women, and more. A Christian university is designed to provide all members of its

---

6. For a good example of this situation in an international student context, see Cynthia Toms Smedley, "Introduction," in *Transformations at the Edge of the World: Forming Global Christians through the Study Abroad Experience*, edited by Ronald J. Morgan and Cynthia Toms Smedley (Abilene, TX: Abilene Christian University Press, 2010) 19–21.

7. Bertrand Russell, *The Scientific Outlook* (New York: Rutledge, 2009) 181.

community with a model of what excellence looks like in the context of each one of those roles and relationships.

While a Christian university can affirm the development of identities such as being a professional or a citizen, it should articulate its goals in broader terms. First, it should cultivate a whole range of human identities such as what it means to be a Christian, a neighbor, a man or woman, future spouse, steward of resources, etc. Second, it should recognize that one's understanding of identities, such as professional or national identity, becomes much richer when placed in the context of a larger story about God's love for us and our complex love for God. For example, career preparation becomes much different if you conceive of it as preparation for a calling or vocation (see chapter 6 for more explanation). Finally, Christian universities recognize that you will need to order your loves regarding your identities. Do you love God, your spouse, your career, or your country first? Unfortunately, secular universities often implicitly and sometimes explicitly order one's loves in ways that run counter to the Christian story. They will send messages that they want you to love a career, knowledge, a country, freedom, critical thinking, leadership, or even their institution (more money, please) more than God.

Of course, we recognize that with the help of the church and Christian mentors, one's multifaceted love of God can be cultivated at a secular university, but the institution is not directly oriented to aid in this endeavor. Both of us were able to grow tremendously in secular university settings. Involvement in Christian groups on campus, the influence of godly Christian staff and professors, and the challenge of being in a secular environment where Christianity did not receive favored treatment sharpened our thinking, affection, and commitments. Yet, this choice also meant missing out on a number of important things that Christian universities provide.

THE EDUCATIONAL AND THEOLOGICAL UNIQUENESS OF THE CHRISTIAN UNIVERSITY

The uniqueness of the Christian university rests on at least three key qualities. First, its leaders believe that education must be holistic in the respect that it addresses issues beyond biblical knowledge or vocations within the church. Bible schools and seminaries do not equip students with the necessary expertise and wisdom to love God in a wide variety of vocations and identity roles outside the church context. While they do play an important role, the Christian university is designed to encompass a much wider set of goals.

Second, universities provide the unique institutional home where both the discovery and transmission of this kind of complex knowledge takes place. Colleges tend to focus on the transmission of knowledge, but a university engages in both endeavors. As one historian of university life said of the first universities: "The universal value of the quest for knowledge and of the transmission of knowledge, which has been recognized ever since antiquity, was . . . given an institutional setting in the university. It has remained so ever since then, even down to our own times; it is the common task, the responsibility—for good or ill—of the universal community of the holders of advanced university degrees."[8] Christian universities join in this search for knowledge with their own set of unique practices, virtues, and ends.

Third, in contrast to secular universities, Christian universities place God and the worship and study of God, particularly theology, at the center of learning. Knowledge and life are viewed as incomplete unless considered in light of God and God's larger story. A Christian university seeks to help students learn what it would mean to be a Christian engineer, business person, or historian, but it also helps them see the quest for knowledge throughout life in the context of God's story. While sorting through difficult issues in class, life as a whole, and especially one's discipline, we need wise guides. A Christian university aims to provide them.

THE CHRISTIAN UNIVERSITY AND THE CHRISTIAN COLLEGE

What is the difference between a Christian college and a Christian university, and why might we now need to expand the idea of the Christian college to the idea of the Christian university? This book addresses the issue throughout its various chapters. Still, it will help to understand the history—both institutions share common Christian roots that stem from their medieval origins, but the university has a more expansive purpose.

The earliest universities emerged out of a unique integration of theological education, liberal arts education, and professional education that occurred in the great cathedral schools found in places such as

8. Walter Rüegg, "Themes," in *A History of the University in Europe: Vol. 1. Universities in the Middle Ages*, ed. Hilde de Ridder-Symoens (Cambridge: Cambridge University Press, 1992) 17–18.

twelfth-century Paris. Their approach to the integration of knowledge helps explain why universities emerged in Western Europe and not in other parts of the world. Scholars in law, theology, and medicine not only received a technical education in their fields, but they also received an education in what were called the liberal arts which meant they also had a command of logic, mathematics, science, and verbal disciplines. Marcia Colish, a noted historian of medieval Europe, writes of this time, "The fact that scientists and philosophers studied in faculties adjacent to theologians trained to raise questions about ultimate values, and that theologians interacted with colleagues in fields not informed by religious criteria, forced all involved to take account of the perspectives and ground rules of other disciplines as well as the disagreements within their own. The scholastics who created this heady educational environment rapidly outpaced monastic scholars as speculative thinkers."[9] These scholars also began to desire new institutional arrangements. Eventually, well-known teachers and clerics started teaching independently of the cathedral schools and monasteries. They became known for innovation and soon formed themselves into guilds of scholars that grew into what would eventually be called *universitas* or universities. The University of Bologna (established at the end of the twelfth century) and the University of Paris (established at the beginning of the thirteenth century) are commonly considered the two earliest universities that eventually became models for other European universities such as Oxford and Cambridge.[10]

While Europeans created universities with up to four different faculties (e.g., theology, law, medicine, liberal arts), American higher education started with more narrowly focused institutions called colleges. To live and be educated in a college was to live together in the place of study instead of in private houses as was the practices of some students at certain European universities. Oxford and Cambridge both used the college model and are still defined by the multiple colleges that come together to form their respective university communities. The early American Puritans who started Harvard in 1636 had graduated from these institutions (mostly Cambridge) and sought to copy its model by starting a single residential college.[11] Similarly, William and Mary (1693) and Yale (1701) started as

---

9. Marcia Colish, *Medieval Foundations of the Western Intellectual Tradition, 400–1400* (New Haven, CT: Yale University Press, 1997) 266.

10. Rüegg, "Themes," in *A History of the University in Europe: Vol. 1*, 6–8.

11. Cotton Mather, *Magnalia Christi Americana* (Hartford, CT, 1820) 2:6–10.

colleges that educated students in the liberal arts in preparation for the ministry. Later, in the mid to late eighteenth century, the First Great Awakening stimulated the establishment of a host of Christian colleges (Princeton, 1746; Columbia, 1754; Brown, 1765; Rutgers, 1766; and Dartmouth, 1769). The Second Great Awakening proved instrumental in giving birth to even more Christian colleges when the number of colleges sponsored by denominations grew from 37 before 1829 to 156 before the Civil War.[12]

While many of these institutions would eventually expand into universities, they initially embodied the liberal arts colleges that dominated higher education in the early United States. These colleges were controlled and funded by Christian groups, required a standard liberal arts curriculum and residential living, and focused more on the teaching of past knowledge than the discovery of new knowledge.[13]

In the late 1800s, however, a new form of institution arose in America that displaced the Christian liberal arts college—the research university. The research university in America was by and large funded by wealthy entrepreneurs and state governments and would eventually take on a largely secular ethos.[14] Whereas evangelical leaders and thinkers dominated the early liberal arts colleges, in the new universities liberal Protestants and later secularists dominated the leadership and scholarship. As a consequence, Christian higher education "was widely regarded as strictly an undergraduate concern."[15] During this era, many of the mainline Protestant Christian colleges also turned in a secular direction.

Only in a smaller group of largely evangelical Christian colleges did Protestant higher education survive. This group emerged partially as a reaction to the liberalism that consumed the mainline schools but their evangelical brand of faith had roots that dated back to Jonathan Edwards as well as the Protestant Reformation. Out of this group emerged a small group of colleges that sought to maintain and cultivate the creative and active integration of faith and learning. Since these institutions were involved

12. Donald G. Tewksbury, *The Founding of American Colleges and Universities Before the Civil War: With Particular Reference to the Religious Influences Bearing upon the College Movement* (New York: Teachers College, 1932) 32–54.

13. William C. Ringenberg, *The Christian College: A History of Protestant Higher Education in America*, 2nd ed. (Grand Rapids: Baker Academic, 2006) 42.

14. See George Marsden, *The Soul of the American University: From Protestant Establishment to Established Nonbelief* (New York: Oxford, 1994); and Mark Noll, *The Scandal of the Evangelical Mind* (Grand Rapids: Eerdmans, 1994) 110–45.

15. Marsden, *The Soul of the American University*, 23.

more in the transmission of knowledge instead of its creation, the integration of faith and learning often involved taking the learning produced in secular research universities and integrating faith into previously created forms of knowledge.

Today, something new is occurring. Christian research universities are developing from the few remaining Christian universities and many Christian colleges are now renaming themselves universities in the light of the fact that they offer a number of graduate programs and degrees. Professors at Christian colleges are also now engaged in the creation of knowledge and are thus inviting their students to join them in those pursuits. As a result, when talking about the Christian university, we will suggest the need to recognize the limitations of the language of the integration of faith and learning and some limitations of relying exclusively upon Christian liberal arts colleges as the Christian ideal for higher education. We should also recognize the limits of separating the two. Delbanco claims, "a college and a university have—or should have—different purposes. The former is about transmitting knowledge of and from the past to undergraduate students so they may draw upon it as a living resource for the future. The latter is mainly an array of research activities conducted by faculty and graduate students with the aim of creating new knowledge in order to supersede the past."[16] In contrast, we suggest that a Christian university will engage in both the transmission and creation of knowledge or learning.

To emphasize these points, we suggest that loving God and others requires Christian universities to focus upon *the creation and redemption of learners and learning*. This mission rests upon the belief, grounded in Genesis 1:27–28, that the Christian's calling entails imitating the model and actions of the triune God in whose image we are made. Theologically speaking, God does not go about integrating faith and learning. Our need to integrate faith and learning stems not from our imitation of God's actions in the Word, but our human limitations—our lack of omniscience and our fallenness. Biblically speaking, however, God is in the business of creating and also redeeming his fallen creation. By understanding their task as creating and redeeming learners and learning, Christian universities undertake the noblest of tasks—imitating and joining in the actions of the triune God.

Christ accomplished this work for us by redeeming the world, reconciling "in himself all things, whether things on earth or things on heaven" (Col 1:20) and restoring God's reign (the kingdom of God). We are also asked to

---

16. Delbanco, *College: What It Was, Is, and Should Be*, 2.

join in that work and the Christian university, following the church's lead, plays a critical role in that process. This redemption involves not only human souls but the rest of God and human creation. When it comes to learning, since our learning faculties and created products are fallen, the redemption of learners and learning entails freeing it from the effects of sin.

This proves particularly important when it comes to learning. Unlike God who created *ex nihilo* or out of nothing, when scholars engage in creational work, they draw not only upon the use of God's natural creation and their own created capacities but also upon a whole set of past creations. In other words, we use terminology, apparatuses, assumptions, data, arguments, resources, languages, etc., provided by others. Scholars build incrementally in reliance on past work. Ideally, such creations would reflect God's plan and purposes. According to this ideal, creating scholarship is not the exact same thing as making or doing scholarship. The creation of scholarship that we have in mind discovers and draws upon God's good created order. Yet, we also know that the fall penetrates, fragments, and distorts all aspects of this work. Therefore, the twin themes of creation and redemption must always be emphasized together.

What makes the Christian university unique is that its faculty members focus not merely upon the creation and redemption of students but they also engage in the creation and redemption of culture as a whole.[17] They seek to add to our knowledge of history, politics, medicine, engineering, nursing, music, and art. Students, in turn, represent the church's next wave of leaders in that process. What better way to help learners understand the creation of culture than to mentor them in the process? What better way to engage in the redemption of academia and academic life?

N. T. Wright, a highly regarded New Testament scholar, received this message as an undergraduate. While at Oxford, he helped organize talks featuring a respected Greek scholar, John Wenham, to address the Christian Union of which Wright was president. He told an interviewer how the talk opened his eyes to the need for Christian scholars:

> In one of those seminars, [Wehnham] said, of course you realize what we desperately need are people who love the Lord and Love Scripture, and have got the academic background to do the Biblical research. He said it's no good waiting for people who don't have

17. See James Davison Hunter, *To Change the World: The Irony Tragedy, and Possibility of Christianity in the Late Modern World* (New York: Oxford, 2010); and Andy Crouch, *Culture Making: Recovering Our Creative Calling* (Downers Grove, IL: InterVarsity, 2008).

that love in their hearts to write silly things about the Bible, and then put Christian scholars to work refuting them. What we need are people out there making contributions and feeding the stuff in to the stream higher up. I guess actually that is the reason I'm doing my work. It struck a chord in me.[18]

Today, Christians increasingly recognize that God created us as image bearers and thus to be co-creators and co-redeemers of culture as well. Faculty members and administrators at Christian universities must endeavor to create learning, learners, and learning communities that enrich God's creation. We need them to nurture Christian professors who can not only engage students in the classroom, but who can also produce scholarship that can influence students outside their own Christian institutions. It was this scholarship that provided tremendous help to us as we sorted through our own intellectual struggles in secular educational contexts. We also need educational institutions where scholars model the creation and redemption of learning to students and do not merely teach students how to integrate faith into learning produced by the secular academy. The Christian university should be designed to play just that role.

QUESTIONS FOR DISCUSSION

1. What were your assumptions about the purpose of attending a college or university? How do they differ from the purposes suggested here for a Christian university?

2. What do you think it means "to cultivate, direct, order, and enrich your loves in the context of our most important relationships and human practices?" How do you believe a Christian university could accomplish this goal?

3. What limited Christian or secular understandings of the university did you perhaps bring to your higher education experience? Why do you think you had those understandings?

4. What is the difference between a Christian college and a Christian university?

18. Tim Stafford, "N.T. Wright: Making Scholarship a Tool for the Church," *Christianity Today* (February 8, 1999) 43.

Chapter One

Learning to Love God

The Christian college refuses to compartmentalize religion. It retains a unifying Christian worldview and brings it to bear in understanding and participating in the various arts and sciences, as well as non-academic aspects of campus life.[1]

—ARTHUR F. HOLMES, *THE IDEA OF A CHRISTIAN COLLEGE*

AARON WAS A BRIGHT student. In fact, he was amazingly bright. He could devour historical, philosophical, and theological texts with the greatest of ease. He not only understood the arguments being made but the intricate details concerning how those arguments were made. Despite the high quality of his undergraduate counterparts, most of them proved to be incapable of keeping up with him. In class, the student union, and the residence hall, he could argue circles around his peers and made for a worthy discussion partner for many faculty members.

Aaron's problem, however, was that his considerable intellectual gifts lacked direction. In more complicated philosophical terms, Aaron's gifts lacked what I will refer to later as a *telos*—a larger commitment that orders how we utilize various gifts, opportunities, and resources in our lives. Aaron and I initially met because he decided he was no longer going to attend chapel. As the dean of students at the time, part of my responsibility was to

1. Arthur F. Holmes, *The Idea of a Christian College* (Grand Rapids: Eerdmans, 1987) 19.

persuade Aaron that chapel attendance was a valuable use of his time. He quickly responded by making arguments that the preaching was poor and that the music was aesthetically displeasing. While I must confess I would certainly agree with him on particular days, the performative quality of these services was a lesser concern to our willingness as members of the body of Christ to come together in a spirit of worship.

Given his *in-attendance*, he was on what our institution referred to as chapel probation. One of the benefits of such a distinction was that he got to spend a considerable amount of time with the dean of students. In the beginning, he was asked (or sentenced—depending upon your perspective) to listen to chapel services he had missed. Given his interest in history, philosophy, and theology, we spent time together discussing the terms of a paper he would compose concerning the role of corporate worship in the lives of Christians. We then had coffee together discussing what he uncovered through his work.

In Aaron, I found a discussion partner who challenged my own thinking. I am hoping the time we spent together challenged his thinking in comparable ways. In the end, our differences proved to be more anthropological than theological. What I mean is that Aaron believed Christians should only participate in worship when they are in the right spirit and thus desire to participate in such an experience. In other words, while Aaron probably believed that learning a subject matter, a sport, or a musical instrument may take continual practice that is undertaken no matter what one feels like doing, he did not think the same about learning to love God. In contrast, Christians throughout history have believed that those moments when they were least inclined to worship God were the moments they needed that reorienting experience the most. Learning to love God with our whole being takes practice. And it should be no surprise that we often do not feel like practicing.

The following chapter makes the argument that in order to truly understand what is at stake in the context of a Christian university, one must first be committed to loving God with one's whole being both as an individual and as part of the larger Christian community. While such love is ultimately a gift or fruit of God's spirit as detailed in Galatians 5:22–23, in order to habitually and continually manifest it in our lives it also requires practice. Just as a team that no longer practices or plays baseball can hardly be called a baseball team, a Christian university that does not engage in corporate practices that nurture our love for God, such as corporate worship, can hardly be called a Christian university.

WHAT IS YOUR (OUR) PURPOSE?

An education, like all critical activities in life, draws upon a larger purpose. It would be odd to see a team practicing the catching or throwing of balls, but then have no explanation for why they thought such a practice was important to perfect. The same proves true in the university. What larger good defines lessons learned in disciplines ranging from anthropology to zoology? What larger good defines lessons learned in arenas such as new student orientation and residence life? More importantly, what larger good sheds light on what kind of relationship those activities, the in-class and out-of-class, share with one another? The unity of the university is found in our relationship to the triune God. The lessons of the curricular (in-class) and the cocurricular (out-of-class) only make sense in the light of a commitment to love God with one's whole being with other members of the Christian faith.

The practice of common worship reminds us of that unity and the fact that the *telos* or purpose of all life is to love God. Everything else is secondary and draws its own orientation from that purpose. Anthropology cannot do that for zoology. Student orientation cannot do that for residence life. Likewise, neither curricular nor cocurricular lessons can define the other. For example, the love, knowledge, and habits cultivated by the practice of common worship grant meaning, purpose, and a right relationship to those areas as well as all other important functions making up the Christian university. These experiences are not designed to be a random composite that occupies students' time in seemingly unconnected ways. In contrast, they are all designed to engage different dimensions of our identity in the larger purpose of loving God.

DIRECTING AND ORDERING OUR LOVES

Augustine of Hippo was arguably the most influential theologian to leave his imprint upon how Christians think about their faith. The North African bishop of the early Christian church was influential in orienting our thinking about the study of Scripture, the nature of the Trinity, and the church's engagement with political power (i.e., the Roman Empire during his time). Despite the prayers of his faithful mother, Monica, Augustine initially chose a different life. During his youth, he lied, stole, and later chased women. He also passionately chased academic prestige and various religions and philosophies. As he describes his journey of desire starting at age nineteen, "we were seduced and we seduced others, deceived and deceiving by various desires, both openly by the so-called liberal arts and secretly in the name of false religion, proud in the one, superstitious in the other, and everywhere vain."[2]

After spending years depending upon the powers of his own intellect and enticed by various distractions, Augustine confessed to God in his classic spiritual autobiography, "our heart is restless until it rests in you."[3] Augustine never renounced his strong passions and desires. He only realized that he needed to find a *telos*, or end that would ultimately satisfy them. In essence, he makes the argument that we human beings are desiring creatures whose affections or loves are constantly in flux until they come to focus on the end for which we are created—an end, or as the Greek philosophers called it a *telos* that can help us order and give direction to our lives. While desires for an education, a career, friendships, and romantic relationships are good, when not properly ordered, they can prove to be distractions instead of noble investments.

Augustine's understanding of the human person stands opposite a conception sometimes presented in some secular contexts which I will call the separate spheres model. For example, at one point in our education, each of us was taught about the wellness wheel. According to the wellness wheel, the sum total of what it meant to be human was subdivided into several different pieces such as the physical and the spiritual as well as the mental and the emotional. Wellness was then defined by granting proper attention to each one as if they are not somehow connected to one another. In the end, however, we likely have a difficult time deciding where our emotional well-being ends and our physical well-being begins.

For Augustine what makes us desiring creatures is the sum total of all that makes us human including what we may refer to as the mental, the emotional, the physical, and the spiritual. In order to be properly focused upon our goal as beings created in God's image, our desires or affections must be focused on God. Distractions to that focus can emerge from any strand of our identity and are unlikely to be singularly identified with just one. For

2. Augustine, *The Confessions*, trans. John K. Ryan (New York: Penguin, 1961) 93.

3. Ibid., 43.

example, is the vice of gluttony (by which I must confess I am greatly tempted when we near a barbecue joint) just a vice emerging from my physical need to eat? If so, why does a heaping plate of smoked brisket tempt me more than a good salad? Part of it likely has to do with taste but part of it has to do with associated memories I have of spending time talking with good friends over such a meal (while I am learning to appreciate a good salad, it is hard to imagine such conversations taking place at a salad bar—no offense intended to my vegetarian friends). At other times, it may ease the pain and frustration of unfulfilled desires about work, relationships, and more. The bottom line is that we human beings are complex beings who rarely, if ever, are defined by only reason, emotion, or physical needs.

Unfortunately, to the detriment of our students modern higher education developed the myth that the mind or rationality is the preeminent dimension of human identity that should be the focus of a university education. According to this model, students come into my class, I pour in the respective facts, they leave, and both parties assume such an exchange is sufficient. Unless I revise my educational assumptions, I might as well refer to students as "brains on sticks" to quote a good friend.

As detailed in the introduction, the biblical narrative challenges us to think more comprehensively about what it means to be human. For example, Christ echoes Deuteronomy 6:5 when he argues the greatest commandment is that we love the Lord with all of our heart, soul, mind, and strength—a commandment recorded by the authors of all three synoptic Gospels (Matt 22:37; Mark 12:30; Luke 10:27). Of course, the second greatest commandment is that we then love our neighbors as we love ourselves. Christ then concludes his admonitions concerning these commandments by indicating that to do so is to be as close to the kingdom of God as one can come this side of eternity. Although it took years of trial and error, Augustine eventually recognized the wisdom of these commandments when he realized true peace comes only when we first love God and then in turn love others.

Prior to our profession of faith in Christ and our baptism, our *telos* remains confused. Like Augustine wrote about in his *Confessions*, we struggle with placing corrupted goods at the center of our lives. Some of us struggle with misappropriating romantic relationships. Some of us struggle with misappropriating professional achievement. Some of us struggle with misappropriating money. However, sex, money, and power are not the only temptations which can misalign our purpose in life. Even a construct as enduringly good as family can become an idol if we place the value of our parents, siblings, spouse, and/or children over our relationship with Christ. Without Christ's influence at the center of our lives, our fallen nature proves capable of turning even good dimensions of creation into expressions of our depravity.

THE BLESSINGS (AND CURSES) OF AN EDUCATION

With this understanding, Augustine also realized that all education cultivates and orders one's loves. The problem with his pagan youthful education was that it disordered his loves. He lamented that his former education "was all that I might succeed in this world and excel in those arts of speech which would serve to bring honor among men and to gain deceitful riches."[4] It also taught him to love the wrong things in the wrong way. He learned to love correct grammar more than eternal salvation. He learned to love "inane tales" more than God's Word. It taught him to strive for academic achievement in order to earn the praise of others rather than to offer praise to God.

In contrast, any community that dares to call itself Christian, including an academic community such as the university, seeks to direct a person's loves toward God. The reason stems from the common *telos* we share that makes us into a common body. In a variety of places in his writings, the apostle Paul refers to the church as the body of Christ and its individual members as parts of that body. For example, in 1 Corinthians 12:27 he writes, "Now you are the body of Christ, and each one of you is a part of it." In Romans 7:4 he contends "So, my brothers and sisters, you also died to the law through the body of Christ, that you might belong to another, to him who was raised from the dead, in order that we might bear fruit for God."

As the embodied continuation of Christ's ministry in the world, the church becomes central in the lives of individuals who profess faith in Christ and seek to live all of their lives in accordance with the commandments he gave. The church's *telos* reorders our lives and then allows us to see the created good in the relationships we share with members of our family and even in more obvious forms of temptation such as sex, money, and power. Given the depraved nature of what it means to be human, we will always struggle with these temptations in one form or another. However, the peace Augustine writes about and our relationship as members of Christ's

4. Ibid., 51.

body allows us to see the true value of our place in this world. If we truly learn to love God then we can learn to love others.

We all share that *telos* in common but the details are different for each one of us. One of the most beautiful glimpses we receive of God's nature comes in the diverse gifts given to those who were created in God's image. In Genesis 1:27 we are told "God created mankind in his own image, in the image of God he created them; male and female he created them." As a result, we each bear that image but it looks different in each one of us. For example, when I was young I desperately wanted to possess the natural gifts necessary to play football. To improve upon the natural abilities I had, I would spend hours in the weight room, doing agility drills, and even running. However, no matter how much time I spent, no college coach ever sent me a letter asking me to consider attending his university on a football scholarship. Truth be told, I barely made a decent junior varsity player in high school. I subsequently needed to learn to appreciate the natural talents given to other young men while also realizing my own talents resided somewhere else.

Although reading, writing, and teaching did not prove to be as enticing a set of gifts to me when I was seventeen, they, in fact, proved to be at the center of what I came to learn to appreciate as my calling. Over time God gave me a passion for ideas and how the communication of ideas can serve as means to help young people realize their full created potential. While my classrooms may not quite generate the fans of an average NFL football game (at least not yet but one always has to have goals) the experiences I have in those settings are ones I find providentially rewarding. Besides, with my level of athletic talent, playing in the NFL (or high school football again for that matter) would simply be an exercise in how many different ways the human body can be hurt.

In addition, our created potential does not just draw upon one strand of our identity but what defines us in full. For example, my calling to serve as a teacher is not something that is simply a cognitive commitment but also something that makes demands upon me in physical, emotional, and spiritual terms in ways I cannot often distinguish from one another. Teaching is thus not just a job but a calling that grants a sense of joy and benefit to me in a number of ways. To simply view it as a job or as an activity that only makes intellectual demands of me would not only shortchange the students I serve but the church that bestowed upon me that calling and the joy God intends for me to receive.

WHY THE CHURCH IS CENTRAL IN ALL OF LIFE

For Christians, the church is the place where we gather together with fellow believers who represent the full array of ways God has endowed people with created potential. Returning to 1 Corinthians, the apostle Paul contends in 12:27–31: "Now you are the body of Christ, and each one of you is a part of it. And God has placed in the church first of all apostles, second prophets, third teachers, then miracles, then gifts of healing, of helping, of guidance, and of different kinds of tongues. Are all apostles? Are all prophets? Are all teachers? Do all work miracles? Do all have gifts of healing? Do all speak in tongues? Do all interpret? Now eagerly desire the greater gifts." In this passage, the apostle Paul indicates that not only does each one of us have a role to play, but also that none of us on our own embodies the diversity of gifts definitive of the body of Christ. Some are called to be apostles. Some are called to heal. Some are called to guide. Of course, I am pleased to read teachers made his list (and note football players did not). In all seriousness, we need one another and we need Christ. In this time and in this place we are all called to fill a role or to embody a particular vocation as a means of loving God and thus also loving our fellow human beings.

As a result of the role that the church plays in the lives of all Christian people, the university that also calls itself Christian must also share a comparable relationship. The vocation of the Christian university is to form within all members of its community the habits of demonstrating love to both God and neighbor in an array of ways reflective of the diverse gifts God bestowed upon members of the created order. For example, my older daughter has a keen analytical mind, a strong commitment to justice, and a penchant for argumentation. While she is only eleven, my wife and I have thought since the day our daughter was born that she was made for politics. Time will tell how her sense of vocation will develop. However, for people with such an array of gifts and a commitment to public service, the Christian university needs to provide them with a distinct set of educational practices that cultivate those talents.

As a result, the array of curricular and cocurricular programs a Christian university offers are to be designed with that *telos* in mind. In essence, in what ways can the study of disciplines ranging from anthropology to zoology create a world reflective of love for God and love for neighbor? In what ways can living in a residence hall and playing on an intramural team cultivate the same commitments? The main way the Christian university is able to implement programs with that *telos* in mind is consistently to reflect upon how the church informs the core of its identity. Any number of other publics will beckon the Christian university to look to them as the means of granting such forms of identity. For example, the nation-state looks to the university to cultivate productive citizens. The business community looks to the university to cultivate the next generation of its leaders. While the Christian university does not disregard the needs of these sectors of society, its first calling is to the church. The *telos* the church grants to the Christian university then becomes the means of determining how it interfaces with these other kinds of communities.

If Augustine's *Confessions* has a rival in terms of defining his legacy, his *City of God* just might be that text. Risking oversimplification, Augustine draws a comparison in this work between what he refers to as the city of God or heaven and the city of man or the earth. As members of the church, Augustine defines the life of Christians as being like a trek through life here on earth to heaven. Referring most definitively to the church as an "alien sojourner," Augustine wants to communicate the idea that Christians are called to be attentive to the needs of the world but their gaze and thus their *telos* is always defined by their destination.[5] In perhaps clearer terms, I often hear students refer to such a way of life as being in the world but not of the world. The church's call to love God grants us a particular perspective that then drives the manner in which we interact with those individuals we are also called to love.

WHAT IS WORSHIP?

You have likely noticed (and rightfully so) that this discussion has in no way yet answered the questions of an astute young man such as Aaron. In essence, what role does chapel or other similar worship practices play in the life of the Christian university? My answer is that practices such as common worship have everything to do with the Christian university. In fact, without the practice of worship of the triune God the very possibility of a Christian university would not exist. Of course, corporate worship does not automatically make the rest of the university Christian. In contrast, our willingness to gather together in common worship is the way we connect with our unique identity as Christian people and thus makes it possible for what we do in a place such as a university to be distinctively Christian or

---

5. Augustine, *The City of God*, trans. Henry Bettenson (New York, Penguin 1984) 761.

to reflect truly the ways those two great commandments of Christ are to be lived out in each one of us.

In his memoir *Hannah's Child*, Stanley Hauerwas, a theologian who served most of his career at Duke University and was once referred by *Time* magazine as "America's Best Theologian" (an honor Hauerwas thought curious at best) argues the church, as mentioned in the preface, teaches us that our lives depend "on learning to worship God."[6] In essence, we cannot know who we are apart from such a practice. In addition, communities are not unlike individuals. They need to be committed to the participation in regular practices that define for them what is most important. As a result, James K. A. Smith, a philosopher at Calvin College, argues in *Desiring the Kingdom* that the Christian university "will extend and amplify the formation that begins and continues in Christian worship."[7]

We first learn to worship in the church. The Christian university then places such a practice at the center of its experience. If, in contrast, a practice such as the study of English or music was placed in the center, the tendency would be to make them idols. The same could be said about placing experiences that take place outside of class at the center (the Lord surely knows frustrated high school athletes like me do not need an excuse to relive the *glory days* through a good game of intramural football). In order to truly love God and love one's neighbor, we must always remember that the first commandment given to Moses was that the people of Israel, people called to strive with God, were to have no other gods before the God who, as recorded in Genesis 20:2, "brought you out of Egypt, out of the land of slavery." Failure to place Christian worship at the center of our lives, and in the case of the Christian university, at the center of our common educational experience is to allow us to run the risk of being re-enslaved to gods of our own creation.

While the call to the Christian university might be the same for any number of educational communities, how it is practiced will vary from campus to campus. One of the key variables in these differences is whether a particular Christian tradition has historically informed the life of and practice of an institution. For example, schools in the Arminian or Wesleyan tradition are much more likely to stress themes of personal holiness than schools in the Reformed or Calvinist tradition that are more likely to

6. Stanley Hauerwas, *Hannah's Child* (Grand Rapids: Eerdmans, 2010) 159.

7. James K. A. Smith, *Desiring the Kingdom: Worship, Worldview, and Cultural Formation* (Grand Rapids: Baker Academic, 2009) 221.

stress themes of human depravity and the sovereignty of God. Those theological themes do make a real difference in terms of how other educational policies and practices are then defined. Regardless, what stands in common should prove to be a commitment to gather together as a community, to hear the Word of God rightly preached, and to participate in the ordinance or sacrament of the Lord's Supper rightly practiced. Other practices such as the offering of praise to God through song also play a role in how a campus community worships. However, the practices of Word and table should rest at the center of what draws a campus community together in an effort to remember the source of its true identity and purpose.

In the end, Christian universities have a commitment to make sure the performative quality of these practices of Word and table are theologically orthodox and engaging to members of the community. However, like I tried to argue with Aaron many years ago, just as important is our commitment as a community to come together in an effort to remember our *telos* in life. Failure to do so unfortunately makes us susceptible to the persuasive voices of any number of lesser gods of our own making. Drawing from the relationship the Christian university shares with the church, the goal of such a place and the people who gather there is to learn to love God and, in turn, learn to love their neighbors. The commitment for all of us is the same. The difference for each one of us then comes in the details of how we are called to demonstrate that expression of love. Even today, I still wonder how Aaron has worked out those details, as his God-given talents were considerable.

QUESTIONS FOR DISCUSSION:

1. Have you ever felt like Aaron in relation to your own chapel experience on campus? Who, if anyone, do you talk with about those thoughts and feelings? What do you think are some important issues for your campus to consider when it comes to the practice of common worship?

2. Do you ever feel like your education has historically emphasized your mind at the expense of other dimensions of your identity? If so, what are some steps you can take to make sure your collegiate education truly engages your full identity as a person created in God's image?

3. Is the church's message concerning the two commandments Christ gave to us to love God and love our neighbor consistent? If so, in what ways? If not, in what ways?

4. If you were to step back and look at your campus as a whole, what would you identify as its *telos*? In a comparable way, what do you view as the *telos* guiding your own life? If those messages are not entirely clear, what could you do on your campus and in your own life to bring such clarity?

5. What does worship look like on your campus? In what way(s) are the preaching of the Word and the practice of the table offered to the community? What role(s) if any, do students play in worship? Administrators? Faculty members?

Chapter Two

Learning to Be Fully Human

*The question to ask about an education is not "What can I do with it?"
but rather "What is it doing to me—as a person?" Education has to do
with the making of persons . . .*[1]

—ARTHUR HOLMES, *THE IDEA OF THE CHRISTIAN COLLEGE*

RECENTLY I SAT AT Starbucks talking with a young man who had attended our university over a decade ago. He faced a number of challenges related to his job, finances, marriage, and more for which he felt ill-equipped. As we talked, he made the observation that his university education, at least when considered simply as career preparation, had really provided him with very little since he had now switched jobs and career paths. Yet, more depressing was his lament, "The university also did little to prepare me to be a dad or a husband or to manage my personal finances."

Actually, I could have echoed his last lament but I would not have considered these things part of the university's job. I chose the secular university I attended as an undergraduate because it had a reputation for producing excellent engineers. My initial understanding of the university is shared by many students, parents, and others. Students complain about general education and see it as something to endure until they reach their major. Numerous parents expect their children to major in something practical that will

1. Arthur Holmes, *The Idea of a Christian College* (Grand Rapids: Eerdmans, 1987) 25.

allow them to obtain a job quickly. I recall a young woman who wanted to explore a variety of areas of interest, but her father pressed her to major in accounting so that she would have an employable skill upon graduation. For this parent, going to college was largely about career preparation. Employers also tend to believe universities should provide students with the vocational skills they need. Even faculty members focus upon providing expertise to students without offering life wisdom. Thus, they will try to diminish general education requirements so students can take more courses in their field or major. All of these approaches reduce the purpose of the university to dispensing educational credentials so a student can get a job.

If we use the biblical analogy of comparing building our lives to building a house, a university that only helps students build their career "room" leaves the rest of the house to the student. It may also promise to help with certain other rooms (e.g., being a good citizen) or certain building skills (we'll help you become a critical thinker). Certainly, as we learn to build our lives we need to obtain certain building skills; however, we also need to think about how to design a "life house" that contains multiple rooms. Supposedly, the contemporary university leaves the design and construction of the foundation to the student.

In reality, all education must build upon some assumed foundation, and for most in the secular university, the city or kingdom we are building together is a liberal democracy and/or a prosperous economy. Thus, secular educators will, with boring predictability, talk about preparing students to be citizens and professionals. Rarely will anyone talk about forming flourishing human beings.

Perhaps the reason is the challenging nature of the task. *The New York Times* columnist David Brooks recently asked people over age 70 to send him essays in which they evaluate their own lives. "Most people," he found, "give themselves higher grades for their professional lives than for their private lives. Almost everybody is satisfied with the contributions they made at work . . . At home, many give themselves mediocre grades."[2] Maybe the universities they attended only prepared them for their professional skills, or possibly these other areas are much more difficult to master.

As the introduction hopefully made clear, what makes Christian higher education different is the view that it should help students gain expertise in areas beyond merely the vocational aspects of their lives. The Christian university seeks to form a student into a well-rounded person who has the

2. David Brooks, "The Life Reports," *The New York Times* (November 25, 2011) 35.

skills, knowledge, and abilities to achieve excellence in every room and in the house as a whole. While we will spend a large part of our lives in the vocational room and the vocational space is an especially complex and important room in our lives, a holistic education offers more. A holistic education addresses questions such as: What's the best overall life design? How do you make sure your job/living room does not take over your whole house? How do you design these other rooms in your life—what might it mean to be a Christian friend, neighbor, citizen, male/female, spouse, parent, and more? A Christian university that is shrinking its general education requirements and/or cocurricular offerings so that it only educates students for a particular professional field is no longer a Christian university. It has become a Christian technical institute.

At their best, Christian universities should attempt to form persons into fully developed human beings. As Arthur Holmes declared, "The human vocation is far larger than the scope of any job a person may hold because we are human persons created in God's image, to honor and serve God and other people in all we do, not just in the way we earn a living."[3] The purpose of the university should be to develop human beings or persons to their full capacity.

WHAT IS A PERSON?

What is a fully developed human "house" or person? Perhaps no question is more important to shaping how a university approaches education. Certain scientific materialists answer this question by claiming a person, similar to a building, is nothing but the physical building materials, brick, mortar, wood and nails, and the mechanical functions the house performs. As a result, when it comes to educating a person, a materialist along these lines will claim, "there is no such thing as 'mind.' It ultimately reduces down to neurons firing and neurochemical transmitter substances flowing across synaptic gaps between neurons, combining in complex patterns to produce something we call *mind* but is actually just brain."[4] This one-dimensional "just" or "nothing but" approach to understanding human persons is not proven by many scientists but assumed. Despite the fact that we experience

3. Holmes, *The Idea of the Christian College*, 25.

4. Michael Shermer, *The Believing Brain: From Ghosts and Gods to Politics and Conspiracies: How We Construct Beliefs and Reinforce them as Truths* (New York: Macmillan, 2011) 22–23.

consciousness, love, and a sense of self, these realities do not count in their scheme as part of what makes us human.

This approach remains tragically one-dimensional because it fails to realize that to describe something physiologically by using one academic discipline does not reduce something to physiology or exhaust our understanding of it. George Marsden, an eminent historian now retired from the University of Notre Dame, discusses how this approach would be like an electrician thinking that the only important aspect of a sign on Broadway reading "LIVE GIRLS" would be the electrical account of the sign's operation. A multidimensional approach would realize its varied significance: "We can imagine a group of sociologists discussing the social significance of the sign. Or next we see a group of economists debating its marketing significance. Experts on gender would see it as essentially about exploitation. Politicians might worry about the controversy it would generate. Ethicists would debate its morality. Linguists might discuss the ambiguity of the syntax. Aestheticians might debate whether it is kitsch or simply tasteless."[5] Interestingly, though Marsden himself is a historian, he leaves out one other key perspective—the historical one. Consider the earlier decathlete illustration that provides a more embodied example. To describe the physiology of a decathlete does not mean we understand every dimension of what it means to be a good athlete. During the Olympics, television networks clearly understand this point. We do not merely hear a doctor describing the physiology of what is occurring during an athletic event. More often, we hear about the larger life narrative and context of a person to understand their motivation and drive—matters not captured by the physiological explanation. Similarly, just as one would describe the house in which they grew up as "nothing but the building materials," a multidimensional approach to the human life would realize its varied significance. Country singer Miranda Lambert sings nostalgically about "The House that Built Me,"

> I know they say you can't go home again
> I just had to come back one last time
> Ma'am I know you don't know me from Adam
> But these handprints on the front steps are mine
> Up those stairs in that little back bedroom
> Is where I did my homework and I learned to play guitar

5. George Marsden, *The Outrageous Idea of Christian Scholarship* (New York: Oxford University Press, 1997) 75.

> I bet you didn't know under that live oak
> My favorite dog is buried in the yard
> I thought if I could touch this place or feel it
> This brokenness inside me might start healing
> Out here it's like I'm someone else
> I thought that maybe I could find myself.[6]

Human beings, just like houses, are more than the materials that compose them. Moreover, as Lambert's song also communicates, we often turn to these human-built structures to somehow find our identity and heal our brokenness.

In contrast, the Christian view of the person should remain multidimensional as the understanding of the person presented in the biblical narrative is multidimensional. To understand what it would mean to develop human persons, Christian universities must consider at least four particular aspects of human personhood discussed in Scripture.

1. Identity Formation: Made in God's Image

Who are we? One of the most important things to recognize, although some people you will read in the university will tell you differently, is that we do not define everything about ourselves. God defines us. The most important of these identities emerges at the beginning of Genesis where God makes an amazing description of human beings.

> Then God said, "Let us make man in our image, in our likeness, and let them rule over the fish of the sea and the birds of the air, over the livestock, over all the earth, and over all creatures that move along the ground." So God created man in his own image, in the image of God he created him; male and female he created them. God blessed them and said to them, "Be fruitful and increase in number; fill the earth and subdue it. Rule over the fish of the sea and the birds of the air and over every living creature that moves on the ground" (Gen 1:26–28).

As this passage reveals, we receive our foremost identity, being made in God's image, from God.

What does it then mean to be created in the image or likeness of God? On one level, it involves exercising the various aspects of God-given capacities. As Scripture indicates, these capacities are multifaceted. The greatest

6. Melissa Lambert, vocal performance of "The House that Built Me," by Tom Douglas and Allen Shamblin, recorded 2010, on *Revolution*, Columbia Nashville.

commandment describes our need to love God with all our heart, soul, mind and strength. Of course, these capacities can be differentiated even more. In *What Is a Person? Rethinking Humanity, Social Life, and the Moral Good from the Person Up*, Christian Smith, a sociologist serving on the faculty at the University of Notre Dame, identifies thirty specific human capacities.[7] These properties include lower-level existence capacities (e.g., conscious awareness), primary experience capacities (e.g., volition, mental representation, understanding of quantity, quality, time, and space properties), secondary experience capacities (e.g., interest formation, emotional experience, and others), creating capacities (e.g., language use, symbolization, creativity, innovation and imagination, composition and recounting of narratives, etc.), and highest order capacities (abstract reasoning, truth seeking, moral awareness and judgment, formation of virtues, aesthetic judgment and enjoyment, and interpersonal communion and love). To participate in the development of humans involves helping individuals cultivate these capacities, especially the two higher-level categories Christian Smith describes, the creating capacities and the highest order capacities.

2. The Image of God and Our Creating Capacities[8]

While a wide range of meanings likely exists about what it means to be made in God's image based upon the context of Genesis 1–11, one biblically faithful interpretation of this phrase indicates that human beings are meant to be the physical representations of God here on earth.[9] Kings in the Near East, such as King Nebuchadnezzar, set up statues of themselves as a symbol of their rule (Dan 3:1). The Bible, by contrast, reveals we are all image-bearers of the King here on earth. Creating and worshiping idols is wrong, not only because it tries to imbue something physical with divine power, but also because it diminishes the honor of the idol worshipers themselves. By creating idols they give up their own status as the representatives of the divine. In this respect, being created in the image of God should be understood primarily as a unique divine calling.

7. Christian Smith, *What Is a Person? Rethinking Humanity, Social Life and the Moral Good from the Person Up* (Chicago: University of Chicago Press, 2010) 54. It should be noted that Smith does not believe his list is exhaustive. In addition, the higher capacities depend for their existence on the lower capacities.

8. I am indebted to Elmer Thiessen for some of the insights provided in this chapter.

9. J. Richard Middleton, *The Liberating Image: The Imago Dei in Genesis 1* (Grand Rapids: Brazos, 2005).

What, then, is our mission that, when fulfilled, will make us more fully developed people? God provides an answer to this question in that just after stating, "Let us make man in our image," God adds "let them rule" over the fish of the sea and the birds of the air, and over all the creatures on the earth (Gen 1:26). This aspect of being created in the image of God is captured in Psalm 8, where the Psalmist asks a poignant question, "What is man that you are mindful of him, the son of man that you care for him? You have made him a little lower than the heavenly beings and crowned him with glory and honor. You made him ruler over the works of your hands; you put everything under his feet: all the flocks and herds, and the beasts of the field, the birds of the air, and the fish of the sea, all that swim the paths of the seas" (Ps 8:4). Men and women are creatures just like the rest of the creatures on earth, but they are also crowned with the glory and honor of being the vice-rulers over the rest of creation.

So important is this notion of humans being created in the image of God that the Genesis account repeats the same point when God calls humans to be fruitful, to increase in number, to fill the earth, and to subdue it (Gen 1:28). This passage is often referred to as the "creation mandate" and is pivotal to understanding human personhood. Just as God, as Genesis 1 demonstrates, is the creator-ruler over all creation, humans are called to be creator-rulers over what God created. Just as there is development in the process of creation, with each creative command leading to a fuller creation, humans are called to develop and create by being fruitful and filling the earth.

Yet, filling the earth involves more than just reproducing. The account of creation found in Genesis 2 gives us a fuller picture of what this assertion might mean. God planted a garden, we are told, and put humans in the garden of Eden "to work it and take care of it" (Gen 2:8, 15). We are to till or cultivate the garden. We are to create, to place our stamp upon God's creation and add to it. We are given the honor of creating culture (essentially the human creations added to God's creation). We name animals and people just as God endowed us with identity. As Smith notes, we create languages and symbols. We create tools, music, and even build cities (all things described in Genesis 4). Humans are called to create civilization and all that it includes. It is no accident that the Bible begins with a garden and ends with a city, the new Jerusalem into which "the kings will bring their splendour" (Rev 21:24).

Yet, we are not merely to exercise our creative capacities without regard for God's creation. God called Adam and Eve not only to subdue the earth, but also to take care of it (Gen 2:15). While the garden provided food for Adam and Eve, God set limits even to this (Gen 2:9, 16–17). Professors who develop students' creative capacities to build culture without considering the house which students are building, forget this important point. After all, advanced creative capacities can be used to build weapons of mass destruction or life-giving medical treatments. The creative capacities that Christian universities seek to develop, such as critical thinking, communication and writing skills, etc., are to help the student create in light of God's overarching story for humanity and creation and the limits expressed about creation's use.

3. The Image of God and Social Identity Formation

Genesis 2, however, indicates that caring for the world and creating are not enough. Naming the animals proves insufficient (Gen 2:19–20). God imbues us with unique identities (e.g., male and female) and allows us to take upon ourselves other created identities. In other words, one of the other aspects of being human involves the social identities we inherit or create and take upon ourselves. After all, Scripture continually reveals God to us through these social roles and images. God's character is revealed through the role of particular professions (e.g., potter, shepherd, teacher). God is also presented to us as a king, parent, a friend, father, and husband. Of course, these images do not at all capture the whole of God just as we cannot be reduced to our human roles.

Still, with humans, our identity also becomes intertwined with these social roles. We inherit roles such as that of being a child, a male or female, and a member of a particular family, race, and nation. We take upon ourselves other identities, such as being a husband/wife, father/mother, a certain profession, members of various social groups, and more. While these identities do not define us completely, they comprise an essential part of who we are. A component of our divine calling is to fulfill those roles creatively and to the best of our ability.

4. The Image of God and Truth, Virtue and Beauty

What is the highest purpose God has for human development? Smith's list of highest order capacities provides us some guidance (abstract reasoning, truth seeking, moral awareness and judgment, formation of virtues, aesthetic judgment and enjoyment, and interpersonal communion and love). These capacities could be neatly summarized as the ability to discern and acquire truth, virtue, and beauty. Again, the acquisition of these three capacities fulfills what it means to be made in God's image.

First, the triune God embodies truth in a personal way. As Jesus said in John 14:6, "I am the way, the truth, and the life." Truth is embodied in Christ, and it is also something embodied in relationships through words, deeds, and being. The professor who demonstrates a love for truth in his or her subject field embodies this capacity in a manner particular to his or her calling. The student who learns to do the same also demonstrates this capacity for truth seeking. This love is expressed at an even higher level when professors and students join together in a common pursuit for truth.

Second, the language of virtue is one of the primary forms of language used to depict God, who is described as "compassionate, gracious, slow to anger, abounding in love and faithfulness, forgiving, just, holy" (Exod 34:6–7). Moreover, just as we are called to create as God created, we are also asked to imitate God by demonstrating God's virtues. The Israelites were told to be holy as God is holy. A central New Testament motif is that Christians should imitate Christ, particularly his self-sacrificial love, but also his forgiveness, servant leadership, humility, and acceptance.[10] If Christian universities seek to develop students to their highest capacities, they must help students cultivate particular virtues, especially love that is properly ordered to the highest truth—the triune God.

Third, beauty or aesthetic judgment also arises from God. As the Psalmist declares, "From Zion, perfect in beauty, God shines forth" (50:2). Similar to the reduction of truth to what might be known through the scientific method, we are often rightly concerned about the reduction of beauty to outward appearances. Nonetheless, we must not despise true beauty in any form. In fact, what Smith describes as aesthetic judgment is something we vitally need, as well as the actual acquisition or creation of true beauty, if we are to bear God's image. French playwright Jean Anouilh claimed through one of his characters in a play, "Beauty is one of the few things that doesn't shake one's faith in God."[11] When an artist, architect, or musician produces something of beauty, he or she reflects both our

10. For more about this emphasis, see John Howard Yoder, *The Politics of Jesus* (Grand Rapids: Eerdmans, 1972).

11. Jean Anouilh, *Becket*, trans. Lucienne Hill (New York: New American Library, 1960) 37.

God-given creative capacities and our ability to embody and extend beauty with God. This kind of beauty draws us out of our self-absorption toward the true beauty found in God and God's creation.

BUILDING A FULLY DEVELOPED HOUSE

Developing our identities often require special callings, creative capacities, and truth, goodness, and beauty. To understand the relationship, it is helpful to consider this idea in the light of one of the most basic identity goals in university life—being a good student who reads critically for truth. I often share my own experience with these themes regarding the simple task of reading. It was not until my sophomore year in college that I realized I did not know how to read. Of course, I do not mean that I did not literally know how to read the words of the page. I learned to love reading as a child and read voraciously throughout my early life and read at a high level when it came to both speed and comprehension. Yet, my failure to read actually involved a deficiency at both a spiritual and intellectual level that my university education helped correct.

The problem was that when I read, I read in a self-centered way. I would not have stated it this way, but I read with the mindset: What relates to my life and interests me? Thus, when my freshman philosophy professor assigned Immanuel Kant and John Stuart Mill, difficult philosophical reading, I did not enjoy it since it was not "fun" reading. I would also read in a self-centered way, dutifully underline those passages I thought striking, interesting, or provocative. Not surprisingly, I received a B- in the course.

It was only later in my university education that I learned to read in an "others-centered" way. I began to ask: What is this person trying to say? What is the person's overall argument? Instead of underlining passages I found interesting, I now began to outline the argument of the book that I thought the author was trying to make. Like a good listener, I would go back and reread passages again to try and understand the writer's argument more accurately. In this respect, I was learning to love my neighbor, the author of the book, by practicing certain virtues we expect in conversation with others, such as patience, accuracy, and charity.

Third, my teachers prodded me to take the third step and ask the question: Is what this writer is saying true, good, or beautiful? I call this the move from others-centered reading to truth-, good-, or beauty-centered reading. Of course, sometimes I had to admit, in humility, that I had no basis by which to judge the author. Yet, in other cases, I began to take my current understanding of truth, goodness, or beauty and begin to wrestle with the author's views. Through this whole process, I developed a range of capacities, such as empathetic reading skills and critical thinking abilities. I also developed particular virtues and a passion for truth, goodness, and beauty. Finally, I understood that these capacities, virtues, and passions were consistent with what it means to be a serious Christian in an academic context.

BECOMING FULLY HUMAN: CREATION AND THE LIBERAL ARTS

God has invited us to come to understand his creation (including ourselves) and develop it. To develop as humans in the four aspects listed above (core identity, creating capacities, social identity, and truth, virtue, and beauty) humans have created forms of curriculum, or systems of knowledge, and educational institutions. This development is really just an extension of our creative abilities given to us by God. Good educational institutions anywhere extend the creation mandate. They enhance our loves, creative capacities, and highest order identities. As they offer good education, they help us to become more fully human in particular areas.

Historical examples abound regarding educational efforts to help us become more human by developing the potential God placed in creation, including human creation. The knowledge of how to extend nature and our own capacities became acquired by individuals and communities with wisdom. Solomon provides an early biblical example and Proverbs 8, in particular, describes the wisdom God instilled in creation. To pass along this wisdom and knowledge, humans wrote books, developed a curriculum, and eventually established formal educational communities.

There is nothing particularly Christian about these activities since we all can learn wisdom from God's gracious creation (Prov; Matt 5:45b; Rom 1:20). Knowledge about the world is dispensed through God's common grace as well and humans throughout the world have reflected the image of God in them by acquiring and distributing knowledge of God's world. In the West, the Greeks, particularly between 450 B.C. and 350 B.C., became known for creating informal schools and systems of knowledge. The best of these discussed how to expand our creative capacities, our ability to pursue and obtain truth, goodness, and beauty, and our understanding of our various social identities and practices (e.g., what it means to be a good citizen or friend).

Later, Roman thinkers such as Cicero, who is the earliest known person to write about the *artes liberales* or liberal arts, expanded upon this tradition. A liberal arts education was initially described as the education of a free man, the leisured person with the time and wealth to contemplate and discuss learning. Seven liberal arts were eventually canonized: the *trivium* (grammar, rhetoric, and logic or dialectic) and the *quadrivium* (arithmetic, geometry, music, and astronomy) although thinkers from the Roman period forward did not necessarily agree upon the number and content of these arts.[12] Past Christians and Christians today defends learning these kinds of arts as helpful for developing the human capacities that God gave us.

This conception of education developed through reliance about creation or natural revelation, but a snake in the educational garden always exists. Due to the fall, humans and human creations always pass along sin in their educational structures. Often, they face the danger of missing important elements and thereby being incomplete and even distorted. This fact occurred with aspects of Greek and Roman education. The particular political context shaped this vision and its content. For instance, the liberal arts of grammar, rhetoric, and logic were skills seen primarily as "crucial in a democratic city-state where winning votes determined the outcome of every question arising both in deliberative bodies, which were concerned with making law, and in judicial assemblies, where forensic presentations were required."[13] A political narrative concerned with power and pride, particularly during Roman times, determined and sometimes distorted educational priorities. Humanity needed a clearer vision of what it means to be fully human and that can guide our educational efforts. The light illuminating this vision appeared in Galilee, a theme discussed in the next chapter.

While most people would deny it, the contemporary university often faces the danger of becoming a technical institute that merely educates students for narrow vocational ends. At best, it provides students with various capacities or tools, so they can learn to build their lives on their own. The young man with whom I spoke had learned some of the life skills he thought he missed using some of the capacities he acquired at the university. Yet, Christian universities can be a bit more honest and helpful. They offer wisdom about the best foundation and how to put your overall house

---

12. Bruce A. Kimball, *Orators and Philosophers: A History of the Idea of Liberal Education* (New York: College Entrance Examination Board, 1995) 29–42.

13. Ibid., 17.

together. They also recognize that they miss their mark if they only provide specialized knowledge necessary to put your vocational room together or only provide general building skills such as critical thinking. They recognize students need an understanding of how the foundation for our lives should be poured and what the blueprint we have inherited means for our purpose in life.

QUESTIONS FOR DISCUSSION:

1. When you first attended a university, did you think its purpose was to provide more than vocational education? What else do you think it should provide?

2. What does it say about the current state of American life when more citizens give themselves higher grades for their professional lives than for their private lives? In what ways might universities be at least partially responsible for that problem? What can the Christian university do to address that problem among members of its community? The world it is called to serve?

3. What does it mean to be a fully developed human being? What are the implications of the one-dimensional or "nothing but" approach to human personhood?

4. What does it mean to be made in the image of God? What aspects of God are we to reflect in our lives?

5. How does the fact that we are made in the image of God help us understand human purpose and the full development of human beings?

6. How were the liberal arts meant to make us more fully human?

Chapter Three

The University's Place
in the Christian Story

To confess God as Creator and Christ as Lord is thus to affirm his hand in all life and thought. It is to admit that every part of the created order is sacred, and that the Creator calls us to exhibit his wisdom and power both by exploring the creation and developing its resources and by bringing our own created abilities to fulfillment.[1]

—ARTHUR F. HOLMES, THE IDEA OF A CHRISTIAN COLLEGE

WHEN I LEFT FOR college, I did not realize I would be faced with a whole set of challenges to my identity. The first semester I quickly faced them. As a baseball player in high school, I thought about walking on to the baseball team in college. I quit after one day when I realized the commitment they wanted was not the commitment I intended to make. Although I was an A student in high school, I failed to make a single A my first semester in college. Although I was a leader in a number of clubs and groups in high school, as a freshman I took my place as an engaged, but new, participant. I suddenly had to face questions about who I was and in what I placed my value. If I no longer was a "baseball player," "an A student," or more, where did I find my identity?

1. Arthur Holmes, *The Idea of a Christian College* (Grand Rapids: Eerdmans, 1987) 21.

My situation was hardly unique. Students attending both colleges and universities undergo a time of tremendous identity formation. They lose identities (e.g., star athlete, first-chair trumpet player, outsider, cheerleader, etc.) and face the prospect of choosing new ones (e.g., joining certain clubs, becoming members of certain living-learning groups, choosing a major, etc.). In this respect, they are tearing down or remodeling parts of their old home and adding new parts. What will provide them a foundation in the midst of this enormous construction upheaval?

I learned that a secure identity foundation starts by reeducating myself about what it means to be made in the image of God and what it also means to be "in Christ." This identity provides the foundation upon which the construction of our other identities and affections takes place. Consider the epistle to the Ephesians (2:19–22) in which the apostle Paul reminds his Gentile readers of their identity in the midst of some identity reconstruction: "Consequently, you are no longer foreigners and aliens, but fellow citizens with God's people and members of God's household, built on the foundation of the apostles and prophets, with Christ Jesus himself as the chief cornerstone. In him the whole building is joined together and rises to become a holy temple in the Lord. And in him you too are being built together to become a dwelling in which God lives by his Spirit." In this respect, Christ provides us more than students often realize. When I ask my students why Jesus came into the world, the usual reply is that Jesus came to save sinners. While biblically accurate (Matt 1:21) the answer demonstrates a limited understanding of Jesus' purpose.

Rarely, do I find a student who states the larger cosmic purpose found in Colossians 1:19. In this passage, Paul describes a grander vision of Christ's work: "For God was pleased to have all his fullness dwell in him, and through him to reconcile in himself all things, whether things on earth or things in heaven, by making peace through his blood, shed on the cross." Jesus Christ not only came to save us from our sins and give us a new identity, he came to demonstrate what it means to be fully God and fully human and to redeem and reconcile humanity and the whole of creation.

As followers of Christ, Christians are charged with sharing with others this comprehensive message of reconciliation. This message focuses not only the good news for the individual but also the implications for the wider human community and God's creation. In other words, Christ's redemptive work encompasses the communities and cultures we create including universities. A university needs this good news, because it also needs a foundational identity by which to orient its education.

The need for such a foundation emerges quickly when a university attempts to organize a general education curriculum or equip students with the creative capacities necessary to enhance their human potential. Consider the capacities associated with being a creator and steward of wealth. C. John Sommerville discusses the problem that emerges when talking to his students about this subject when he taught at the University of Florida. "The way I put it to my students is to ask where in the university they would go to learn how to *spend* their money. We have lots of programs that tell you how to make money and be useful to the economy. But where would you go to learn how to spend your money intelligently? That is, where does one learn what is *valuable in and of itself?*"[2] A foundational identity provides the basis by which an educational institution could actually answer that question.

Educational institutions, implicitly or explicitly, always pass along an understanding of what identity or identities it thinks are most important for students. One of the easiest ways to see this is to look at what history courses are required in its general education. What is the connection? History provides one of the primary ways we get to know our identities. If you want to get to know someone, you can ask them their favorite colors, foods, and sports teams; ask their political opinions; and more. However, one of the most important things you can learn is the person's story. It gives you tremendous insight into who he or she is as a person. The same proves true with the stories of groups, institutions, countries, and more.

A Christian university should start by educating students about their foundational identity—an identity they discover by immersing themselves in the Christian story. In other words, the foundation of Christian education comes from God and its vision of human development originates from the fact that humans are made in God's image. Furthermore, Christian students must be reminded that their foundational identity within God's larger narrative rests in Christ.

The most natural place for such discovery to take place resides in foundational classes within each discipline, especially classes about Scripture and theology. Unfortunately, the reduction of education to the life of the mind by university professors often means that they do not conceive

2. C. John Sommerville, *The Decline of the Secular University* (New York: Oxford University Press, 2006) 8.

of foundational courses, such as Christian Scripture, as identity formation courses. Instead, they are understood primarily as introducing students to academic conversations about Scripture. What professors may fail to communicate to students is that one's fundamental identity and identity community radically alters how one even sees, reads, and interprets Scripture. Turning again to the Epistle to the Ephesians, the apostle Paul writes to those "in Christ," that they are to no longer live like those "darkened in their understanding and separated from the life of God because of the ignorance that is in them due to the hardening of their hearts" (4:18). Instead, they are to "put off [their] old self, which is being corrupted by its deceitful desires; to be made new in the attitude of [their] minds; and to put on the new self, created to be like God in true righteousness and holiness" (4:22–23). Our new identity in Christ restores the image of God in us and reshapes our whole being, including our desires and our interpretive lenses through which we evaluate all knowledge.

In this respect, the Christian university must also cultivate Christian identity in a different way than the church (which also offers teaching about Scripture) and the secular university. It seeks to cultivate this identity within the full range of academic fields and the whole sphere of human learning. One of the ways it can accomplish this endeavor is to require every student to take a course in post-biblical church history, something the church rarely provides. The importance of such an approach rests on the fact that we understand identity through stories. If Christians are fundamentally citizens of God's kingdom and thus identified with the worldly representation of that kingdom, the church, they should seek to learn the church's story. Interestingly, a study of Christian colleges and universities found more schools required students to take classes about United States history or Western civilization than about post-biblical church history.[3] In other words, they are more focused on making sure students know the Western or American story than the story of the church. This represents a major failure of the Christian university in terms of the *telos* or purpose of the education it seeks to provide. They are captured and enthralled with another lover and story.

The reason why such a course proves important is because it helps us see how the church has sought to join with God's redemptive work in

3. Perry L. Glanzer and Todd Ream, "Whose Story? Which Identity? Fostering Christian Identity at Christian Colleges and Universities," *Christian Scholar's Review* 35 (2005) 13–27.

various spheres of culture throughout history. For example, the early church faced important questions such as: "What does the redemption of human callings look like in marriage, work, and political citizenship?" Another important question for the early church was, "What are the implications of following Christ for education?" Answering these questions was inescapable since Christ's Great Commission reveals that educational tasks such as making disciples and teaching are fundamental tasks in which followers of Christ engage (Matt 28:18–20).

EDUCATIONAL VISIONS IN THE EARLY CHURCH

When the early church began building its own educational tradition to accomplish these tasks, it faced the challenge of how developing this new Christian revelation should interact with Greek and Roman thinking. They had to ask, as the early Christian thinker Tertullian did, "What indeed does Athens have to do with Jerusalem?"[4] Various church fathers gave three types of answers to this question. First, some rejected large parts of pagan learning as too corrupt. Tertullian's famous quote comes from a work in which he argued that "heresies are themselves instigated by philosophy . . . Our instruction comes from the porch of Solomon, who had himself taught that the Lord should be sought in simplicity of heart. Away with all attempts to produce a Stoic, Platonic, and dialectic Christianity!"[5] His approach, as others like it, found biblical inspiration in 1 Corinthians 1:20–25 where the apostle Paul asked:

> Where is the wise man? Where is the scholar? Where is the philosopher of this age? Has not God made foolish the wisdom of the world? For since in the wisdom of God the world through its wisdom did not know him, God was pleased through the foolishness of what was preached to save those who believe. Jews demand miraculous signs and Greeks look for wisdom, but we preach Christ crucified: a stumbling block to Jews and foolishness to Gentiles, but to those whom God has called, both Jews and Greeks, Christ the power of God and the wisdom of God. For the foolishness

---

4. Tertullian, "On Prescription against Heretics," in *Ante-Nicene Fathers, Vol. 3, Latin Christianity: Its Founder, Tertullian*, edited by Alexander Roberts and James Donaldson (Peabody, MA: Hendrickson, 1995) 246. See: http://www.ccel.org/ccel/schaff/anf03/Page_246.html.

5. Ibid., 246. See: http://www.ccel.org/ccel/schaff/anf03/Page_246.html.

of God is wiser than man's wisdom, and the weakness of God is stronger than man's strength.

Defenders of this position pointed out how human reason failed to appreciate the uniqueness of God's plan in Christ. It is easy to find other possible contrasts. For example, while the pagan liberal arts was an education for a free man, a Christian education was designed for people who had chosen to be "bondservants of Christ" and thus did not pursue the wealthy or leisured life of contemplation. The two purposes appeared to be at odds.

A second group of church fathers saw certain Greek philosophies, particularly Platonism, Aristotelianism, and Stoicism (as found in later Roman writers such as Cicero) as consistent with, and even building blocks for, Christian faith. For instance, Justin Martyr wrote:

> For while we say that all things have been produced and arranged into a world by God, we shall seem to utter the doctrine of Plato; and while we say that there will be a burning up of all, we shall seem to utter the doctrine of the Stoics: and while we affirm that the souls of the wicked, being endowed with sensation even after death, are punished, and that those of the good being delivered from punishment spend a blessed existence, we shall seem to say the same things as the poets and philosophers . . .[6]

Justin contended that these similarities in beliefs stem from the fact that the human mind understands reality by participation in the universal *Logos*, the Greek word for both "word" and "reason." In other words, there is a universal reason and order to the world everyone can discover. He went on to note that the author of the Gospel of John describes Jesus as the *Logos*, the "word" made flesh, and concluded that Christ embodied God, the universal reason behind the world.

Similar connections between the Gospel of John and Greek thinkers were made by others. For example, in the *Republic*, Plato described the journey to true knowledge as like one that takes you from the darkness and shadows of a cave to the glorious light of the sun. Christians found in this image similarities to John's description of Jesus as the light of the world. Furthermore, they argued that in a student's journey from the darkness of the cave to the light revealed by God in Christ, students had best start with pagan truth so that their eyes could learn to adjust to the bright light of revelation found in Christ (similar to the way that one is initially blinded

6. Justin Martyr, *The First Apology of Justin Martyr*, trans. Roberts-Donaldson, (http://www.earlychristianwritings.com/text/justinmartyr-firstapology.html) ch. 20.

when coming out of a cave). Thus, one finds in St. Basil's *Address to Young Men* this admonition:

> Just as dyers prepare the cloth before they apply the dye . . . so indeed must we also, if we would preserve indelible the idea of true virtue, become first initiated in the pagan lore, then at length give special heed to the sacred and divine teachings, even as we first accustom ourselves to the sun's reflection in the water, and then become able to turn our eyes upon the very sun itself.[7]

According to this approach, Christian students should actually start by studying select pagan writers and only later turn their eyes upon the full light of the gospel.

This second model found additional biblical inspiration in the wisdom literature and the figure of Solomon. After all, they noted that Solomon, as traditionally believed to be depicted in Proverbs and Ecclesiastes, used his reason to study the world, discovered wisdom by observation, and came to see the futility of a life without God and the importance of God and God's revelation. Similarly, the use of reason, they insisted, could lead the wise pagan to such conclusions. Once convinced of life's futility and brokenness, students would understand their need for God's ultimate revelation in Christ.

A third view held that pagan education must be fully reinterpreted through the lens of faith if one is to truly seek understanding. Exemplifying this view in the *Confessions*, Augustine looked back over his life through faith and then understood the road on which God led him. God did use pagan thinkers, such as Plato and the Roman Stoic philosopher Cicero, to lead him to Christ, but he could only understand this later. Moreover, he could only properly interpret things such as his old pagan schooling, pagan thinkers and his own desires for fame, academic glory, and sexual fulfillment, after examining his life through the lens of faith.

This third model found biblical inspiration in various teachings of Jesus but also throughout the Epistles. In letters such as Romans, Galatians, Ephesians, and Colossians, the first parts of the books do not contain commands about how to live (e.g., Rom 1–11; Gal 1–4; Eph 1–3; Col 1–2). Instead, they describe the implications of God's story, particularly the work of Christ, for how we should understand our identity. Only by considering the world in light of Christ's redemptive story and one's identity in Christ, can

---

7. Basil, "Address to Young Men," in *Three Thousand Years of Educational Wisdom*, ed. Robert Ulich (Cambridge, MA: Harvard University Press, 1999) 154.

one truly understand how to think and live. Thus, only in the last portions of those letters are instructions given about how Christians should live.

In education, those operating with this third view saw the need not merely to add Christian teaching to pagan learning but to begin education by letting the Christian story transform the whole of the liberal arts. Hugh of St. Victor, an eleventh-century-Christian educator whose work will be described at length later in this book, provides an example of this approach. In the beginning of the *Didascalion: A Medieval Guide to the Arts*, he set forth a vision of education's end that is shaped by the biblical narrative instead of a political narrative (as was particularly common to the educational tradition inherited from the Romans):

> This, then is what the arts are concerned with, this is what they intend, namely, to restore within us the divine likeness, a likeness which to us is a form but to God is his nature. The more we are conformed to the divine nature, the more do we possess Wisdom, for then there begins to shine forth again in us what has forever existed in the divine Idea or Pattern, coming and going in us but standing changeless in God.[8]

For Hugh, education in the liberal arts should help us restore the marred image of God and become fully human. Furthermore, Hugh believed that in order to recover the wisdom God can provide we need to study both God's work of creation and redemption. After all, he wrote, "In this were the wise men of this world fools, namely that proceeding by natural evidences alone and following the elements and appearances of the world, they lacked the lessons of grace."[9] He called both the study of God's work of creation and redemption "philosophy" (which included theology) and suggested that philosophy is the discipline which investigates human and divine things comprehensively and draws upon both natural reason and revelation for guidance. Theology in his view was the peak of philosophy and the perfection of truth. Hugh's vision of Christian education, as well as other Christians during this time, would prove instrumental in the eventual creation of the first Christian universities, an incredible development in the history of education.

8. Hugh of St. Victor, *The Didascalion of Hugh of Saint Victor: A Medieval Guide to the Arts*, trans. Jerome Taylor (New York: Columbia University Press, 1991) 61.

9. Ibid., 35.

THE MEDIEVAL UNIVERSITY: THE CREATION AND FALL OF A CHRISTIAN INSTITUTION

One of the interesting questions of history is: Why did universities start in the Christian, specifically Catholic Western, part of Europe? In other words, why is it, as argued by noted sociologist Rodney Stark, that "the university was a Christian invention"?[10] In fact, historically speaking, Christian universities served as "the mind of the Church"—the place where Christians, as image bearers of God, have searched out God's truth in every area of knowledge and practice, and transmitted deeper forms of wisdom. One of the reasons for this historical development stems from what scholars have noted about the understanding of God and the world communicated particularly in Western Christianity, which "depicted God as a rational, responsive, dependable, and omnipotent being and the universe as his personal creation, thus having a rational, lawful, stable structure, awaiting human comprehension."[11] This understanding of God led to unique scientific and educational developments not initially found in China, India, the Middle East, or even the Christian East.

The degree to which human reason, unaided by the divine revelation of the Scriptures and the interpretive help of the church community, could actually discover God's created order proved the most vital question. Unfortunately, certain answers also contained the seeds that would birth a prideful rejection of the Creator. As medieval universities developed in the late twelfth and early thirteenth centuries, a critical decision was made. Instead of seeing philosophy as dependent upon both natural reason *and* revelation and thus critically integrated with theology, as the third approach above envisioned, a sharper distinction began to be made between philosophy (the sphere of natural reason) and theology (that guided by special revelation) that reflected the second approach above.

As a result, philosophy in a narrow sense (the sphere of natural reason that does not include theological truths discovered by special revelation) became the foundation of the university education instead of philosophy in the broad sense used by Hugh of St. Victor (which includes revelation). This view partly stemmed from the belief that one needed the learning

---

10. Rodney Stark, *For the Glory of God: How Monotheism Led to Reformations, Science, Witch-Hunts and the End of Slavery* (Princeton, NJ: Princeton University Press, 2003) 62.

11. Ibid., 147.

supplied by the whole range of liberal arts (philosophy broadly defined) to interpret Scripture properly.

The problem with this approach as it became practiced in the medieval university was that it treated theology, specifically theology derived from special revelation in the Scriptures, as the roof of the building of human learning instead of the foundation. With this practice, students in the university started with the liberal arts and philosophy became the initial subject (although it should be noted that some of the philosophical subjects of the day would be considered theology today). Theological faculties where students studied theology grounded in the Scriptures were found only in special full universities and were reserved for the more advanced students.

The result was that a significant amount of confidence became invested in how reason and general revelation, apart from Scripture and later the church, could guide students, especially when used in conjunction with particular creative capacities of humans. Because a Christian narrative and understanding of the world dominated the mindset of the time, it was assumed that students would reason about nature (natural philosophy) or proper social relationships (moral philosophy) within the overarching narrative or worldview of Christianity. Furthermore, it was taken for granted that everyone believed we were all made in God's image and that reason and faith could be complementary in cultivating that image.

The Protestant Reformers complained about this overreliance upon reason and pagan philosophers in the universities of their time. In his address *To the Christian Nobility*, Martin Luther famously wrote, "What are [the universities] but places where loose living is practiced, where little is taught of the Holy Scriptures and Christian faith and where only the blind, heathen teacher Aristotle rules far more than Christ? . . . his book on ethics is the worst of all books. It flatly opposes divine grace and all Christian virtues, and yet is considered one of his best works. Away with such books! Keep them from Christians."[12] Luther's views, however, did not characterize Protestants as a whole. In fact, Luther's suspicions about pagan authors and the role of natural revelation were not held by his successor, Philip Melanchthon, or another important reformer, John Calvin.

Consequently, the Lutheran, Calvinist, and Anglican universities did little to alter the trend of placing philosophy (defined in a way that excluded theology and sacred writings) as the foundation of university education

---

12. Martin Luther, *Three Treatises*, trans. Charles M. Jacobs (Philadelphia: Fortress, 1970) 93.

and treating theology and sacred writings as the pinnacle or roof of learning. Eventually, the view would emerge that universities could easily remove and replace the roof. What they did not realize is that they were really trying to replace the foundation.

THE RISE OF THE SECULAR UNIVERSITY

American higher education could have proved an exception. While the number of universities actually declined by two-thirds across Europe in the eigteenth and nineteenth centuries, Protestants successfully multiplied Christian liberal arts colleges in America.[13] Unfortunately, they kept the basic structure of the medieval university and continued the trend of marginalizing theology. While a more radical model that placed theology at the foundation of the university was proposed by a few Puritans who influenced the founders of Harvard, it never actually became an alternative model either in Europe or America. Consequently, students were increasingly taught courses in natural and moral philosophy that were expected to lead them to Christian convictions using reason apart from revelation. Nonetheless, such classes usually assumed the guiding Christian worldview was revealed through the Scriptures.

The primacy of the use of natural reason and philosophy as the foundation meant that secularization could occur much more easily. When an alternative secular narrative started to emerge through the spread of Darwinism (which led some to view the evolutionary process as unguided by any larger designer), professors in the fields of natural philosophy and moral philosophy started to abandon the Christian foundations that had been implicitly present. In this way, they secularized philosophy and the liberal arts. Out of these secularized disciplines grew psychology, sociology, economics, and a whole range of disciplines, many of whose original theorists, such as Sigmund Freud, Herbert Spencer, Auguste Comte, and Karl Marx, had anti-religious views.

Furthermore, when advocates of a research university that valued specialized research and professional preparation started to emerge in

---

13. Walter Rüegg, "Themes," in *A History of the University in Europe: Vol. III, Universities in the Nineteenth and Early Twentieth Centuries*, ed. Walter Rüegg (Cambridge: Cambridge University Press, 2004); Donald G. Tewksbury, *The Founding of American Colleges and Universities before the Civil War: With Particular Reference to the Religious Influences Bearing upon the College Movement* (New York: Teachers College, 1932).

Germany and then sent their disciples to America, the old Christian colleges found themselves without the theological resources and flexibility to deal with their new idea of the university. George Marsden recounts how past leaders of Christian colleges such as Yale "could defend what they already had, the disciplined undergraduate college as a haven against secular intrusion, but they had no real plan for the university as a graduate, professional, or specialized scientific institution."[14] Without a plan for a Christian university, leaders of older Christian colleges simply transformed their institutions into secular research universities.

Part of the problem was that the leaders equated the old prescribed classical curriculum, which included subjects such as Latin and moral philosophy, with their defense of Christianity. Instead of being creative and devising a new curriculum and university structure that framed professional and scientific studies theologically, they became conservative about a curriculum that was largely meant for training clergy and conserved elements not always central to cultivating the full humanity of everyone.

Yet, the move to a secular university also threatened the old vision of education as humanization described by Hugh of St. Victor. If the university no longer believed in the Christian narrative or the belief that humans were made in God's image, they had to find a new view of humanity and a new guiding story. While Darwinian evolution's optimistic promise of progress provided that new story, when divorced from a purposeful God it provided no specific vision of what it means to be a fully developed human being. As noted historian C. John Sommerville observed. "When American universities became officially secular, a century ago, the problem of defining the human was not foreseen. Much of a traditional Christian intellectual culture was taken for granted. Mistaking the habits of thinking for rationality itself, those founders thought religion was redundant and could be ignored without loss of substance."[15] The result is that the human capacities—views of truth, goodness, or beauty—or social identities that a university should seek to enhance in students become confused and often quite limited.

Today, secular universities no longer seek to form human persons. In other words, they no longer understand humans as made in God's image to exercise specific creative purposes, to fulfill a wide range of God-ordained identities, and to pursue specific understandings of the true, good, and

14. George Marsden, *The Soul of the American University* (New York: Oxford, 1994) 128.

15. Sommerville, *The Decline of the Secular University*, 24.

beautiful. Instead, they supposedly ignore the foundations of what it means to be a person and only offer limited parts of the four aspects of personhood described in chapter 2.

Consider the comprehensive vision outlined by former Harvard University President Derek Bok in his book, *Our Underachieving Colleges*.[16] First, Bok provides no foundational understanding of what it means to be a person, as there is no overarching understanding of personhood that can hold everything together. Second, he reduces the role of the university in the other three areas of personhood. When it comes to creative capacities, he merely lists five: 1) learning to communicate; 2) learning to think; 3) living with diversity; 4) preparing for a global society; and 5) acquiring broader interests. While Bok's approach is actually more expansive than the views of many secular educators because he includes "building character" as an aim of the college, he actually undermines this role with claims such as, "It is not the place of faculty members to prescribe what undergraduates ought to consider virtuous."[17]

With regard to social roles or callings, Bok only indicates that the university should help students with two: 1) preparation for citizenship; and 2) preparation for a career. Finally, Bok never mentions the need to pursue truth, goodness, or beauty. In this view the contemporary university is not about directing one's love toward these ideals or the God who fully represents them. This approach provides students with a fragmented form of general education. As Arthur Holmes noted, "It does nothing to unify a person or his view of life, and it might well encourage the view that life has no overall meaning at all. It simply creates a connoisseur of the fragments of life. But a jack of all trades is a master of none, a fragmented education."[18] A university needs a more unified vision of the person if it hopes to provide a unified and holistic approach to human development.

Education within the Christian story must take place in a more transformative manner than most Christian colleges and universities recognize and practice. As mentioned earlier in the chapter, Christ came not merely to save individual sinners but to redeem the whole world, including the world of learning. This vision of redemption requires that a Christian university

---

16. Derek Bok, *Our Underachieving Colleges: A Candid Look at How Much Students Learn and Why They Should Be Learning More* (Princeton, NJ: Princeton University Press, 2006) 67–81.

17. Ibid., 150.

18. Holmes, *The Idea of the Christian College*, 27.

offer students opportunities and help in discovering, constructing, and maintaining an identity story. The Christian university should model what it means to order the importance of one's identities and thus order one's loves. The final goal of transformation is not only for students to learn the Christian story, but also to realize that the story of the Christian church is their primary communal and individual identity. As part of getting to know the church's story, the role of the Christian university must involve introducing students to the Christian intellectual tradition. If a student attends a Christian university and does not gain an understanding of how being a Christian transforms learning, the Christian university has failed to live up to its identity and purpose.

QUESTIONS FOR DISCUSSION:

1. What identities have you discarded and taken upon yourself while in the university?

2. How can the Christian university cultivate someone's Christian identity?

3. What are the implications of Christ's redemptive work for God's creation as a whole as well as human creation (i.e., culture)?

4. What are the three different approaches that the early church used when approaching pagan learning? Which one do you find most persuasive?

5. Why did the view emerge that philosophy described all of learning and that theology could be understood as the roof of learning? How did this view lead to the secularization of the medieval universities?

Chapter Four

The Creation and Redemption of Learners and Learning

[The person with a Christian worldview] explores the creative and redemptive impact of the Christian revelation on every dimension of thought and life.[1]

—ARTHUR F. HOLMES, *THE IDEA OF A CHRISTIAN COLLEGE*

DENNIS PRAGER, A JEWISH author and talk show host in Los Angeles, regularly asks high school seniors who they would save first if they saw their dog and a stranger drowning. In the fifteen years he has asked the question, two-thirds of the students from public schools said they would not save the stranger first. Usually, students justify their decision by saying that they love their dog but do not even know the stranger. Prager concludes, "They have been raised on love as their only value." They also likely have been educated in a naturalistic view of evolution that leads to the obvious conclusion "that we are one species among many, with no claim to special status."[2]

---

1. Arthur Holmes, *The Idea of a Christian College* (Grand Rapids: Eerdmans, 1987) 58.

2. Steve Stewart-Williams, *Darwin, God and the Meaning of Life: How Evolutionary Theory Undermines Everything You Thought You Knew* (New York: Cambridge University Press, 2010) 186.

Prager consistently receives different answers from seniors at religious schools. He finds they "believe that humans are created in God's image and dogs are not."[3] Consequently, students reason that even though they love their dog more than a stranger, they would save a stranger before their dog. As this example illustrates, the fact that humans are made in God's image changes everything about how we love. We order our loves and thus resolve the conflicts between competing loves differently. When we face conflicts between the objects of our affections such as love for our family, our job, friends, dog, sports team, country, and more, we will and should love in a unique way.

Higher education proves no different. As image bearers of God, we love advanced learning because it fulfills essential purposes for which we are designed. It helps us acquire the wisdom of the God in whose image we are made. It can foster a deeper love for God and God's creation in ways that contribute to greater human flourishing (including our own). It does this by enhancing our human capacities to join with God in *the creation and redemption of learners and learning*—a purpose which we have argued should be one of the distinct purposes of the Christian university. Of course, God is ultimately the one who creates and redeems learners and learning, but we are also asked to join with God in these tasks.

As mentioned in the introduction, this language is somewhat different than that used at many Christian colleges and universities. Arthur Holmes proclaimed in *The Idea of a Christian College* that a distinctive of the Christian college "should be an education that cultivates the creative and active integration of faith and learning."[4] Why do we now propose a different language? The foremost reason is theological, while many of our other reasons are linked to the problems one finds with integration language when one goes from applying it within a college setting to applying it within a university setting.

First and most important, this language focuses on the way Christian educators should bear God's image in the midst of education, particularly in advanced forms of education found in the university. In other words, this language communicates the Christian learner's highest calling to imitate the model and actions of the triune God. One could claim the same for

3. Dennis Prager and Jonathan Glover, "Can We Be Good Without God? A Debate between Dennis Prager and Jonathan Glover at Oxford University," *Ultimate Issues* 9 (1993) 13.

4. Holmes, *The Idea of a Christian College*, 6.

integration. Arthur Holmes even suggested, "Integration is a task never fully accomplished by anyone but God himself."[5] As mentioned in the introduction, we do not believe God goes about integrating faith and learning. Our need to integrate faith and learning stems not from our imitation of God's actions in Scripture, but our human sinfulness. Only in a fallen world, does learning become secularized, so that faith and learning must once again be integrated. Fortunately, God is in the business of creating and also redeeming his fallen creation. By understanding our task as creating and redeeming learners and learning, we as educators and learners truly become image bearers of God.

Second, when used in the university, the language of "integration of faith and learning" creates narrow conceptions of the Christian scholar's task as well as the Christian student's calling. When scholars or students "integrate faith and learning," they have already admitted that the original learning or culture humans created failed to demonstrate "faith" and therefore the faith must now be integrated. Certainly, learning must be redeemed. Yet, this way of speaking fails to acknowledge that Christians, especially in the university, should be involved in creating learning.

Third, an advantage of rearticulating the Christian scholar's or student's task in this manner is that it may help reshape views about the limited relationship between Christianity and disciplines not always seen as amenable to integration, disciplines often found in the university (e.g., music, chemistry, engineering, mathematics, architecture, computer science, etc.). Asking how one integrates faith into music or chemistry may sound like a difficult question. In contrast, if one thinks about the creation of music or the creation of learning about engineering, architecture, or chemistry, it is easy to think about the productive discussions and directions such conversations might take. For example, consider the question: How can an architect creatively design a home or a civil engineer creatively construct a highway system so that it maximizes human flourishing and stewardship of God's creation? Answering this question requires the complex skills and demanding thinking that the Christian university can and should provide.

5. Ibid., 45.

THE CREATION AND REDEMPTION OF ADVANCED LEARNERS: IT'S COMPLICATED

God made us learners. For an example, watch an infant. A baby naturally explores, experiments, and makes great efforts to learn about and make sense of his or her world. God also made us diverse and distinctive kinds of learners in that he endowed each of us with particular natural gifts and innate desires, such as a mathematical capacity, a musical ear, or something else entirely.

Humans created educational institutions to extend and refine our God-given curiosity and these natural desires, capacities, and gifts. In fact, one of the great joys of life is that we can join with God in the continued creation and development of advanced learners. One might even find universities with the stated goal of creating "lifelong learners." Of course, creating advanced learners is complicated. As with every practice in life, learning involves initiating the novice into the various aspects necessary to achieve mastery in that particular area. The following section describes ten dimensions that must be cultivated when helping students become learners.

1. Story and setting. What is the larger story and setting in which education takes place? Establishing these two things is crucial for a variety of reasons when creating advanced learners. First, it gives meaning and drama to the endeavor. My son instinctively knows this point when he engages in the practice of basketball. When we start playing in the driveway he asks, "Dad, what team are you going to be?" He wants to place the practice in an already existing story to give it purpose and excitement. He pretends it is the NBA Finals. Christians know there is a metanarrative that gives learning meaning and motive to learning. The fact that God, God's kingdom, and Satan exist will also influence our understanding of the setting for learning.

2. Gifts/abilities. To be excellent in any practice, one must have the necessary abilities and gifts. Just as I described in chapter one my recognition that high-level football requires particular gifts (and ones I did not have) one needs certain capacities to become excellent in learning. Yet, we must also again acknowledge the wonderful diversity of human gifts and abilities that contribute to learning.

3. Ends or purpose. The most basic thing to learn about any practice, including learning, is the ultimate purpose or *telos*, a point discussed earlier in chapter 1.

4. Specific rules and principles. You cannot play a game without knowing the rules. A marathon runner who does not run the full distance of the race cannot be considered a true athletic champion. Learning also has similar rules since a real learner does not take short cuts (e.g., cheating on an exam, plagiarizing papers, etc.). These standards are shared by both secular and Christian universities. Every American university, no what matter what type of relativism may be taught in a class, still expects all students not to cheat, plagiarize, falsify research results, etc.

5. Virtues and vices. Virtues are the character qualities necessary for the successful practice of learning (e.g., self-control, honesty, creativity, critical thinking). Vices are those behaviors that undermine it (laziness, dishonesty, lack of imagination, shoddy or simplistic thinking).

6. Practice. Acquiring virtues requires, among other things, God's grace and practice. We must hone our whole being, including our senses, similar to that of an athlete or a musician. A trained musician experiences an opera much differently than someone untrained in music. A tennis coach can see and observe things that someone who rarely plays tennis will never see. The famous Christian educator from the seventeenth century, Jon Amos Comenius, said, "The learned must possess hands, tongue, eyes, ears, brain, and all internal and external senses different from the masses . . . For this reason they are reshaped, and this cannot be done without toil and pain."[6] Malcolm Gladwell, a best-selling journalist, has claimed that in order to become good at something, one needs to practice it for 10,000 hours.[7] Yet, he cautions that practice is often insufficient, because one can continually practice doing the wrong thing and develop vices or bad habits. Consequently, one needs something more than practice.

7. Teachers/coaches/mentors. To know how best to practice and correct your mistakes, you need teachers. After all, even the best athletes in the world require coaches. Christian universities recognize the triune God as the ultimate mentor. The Bible particularly talks about the Holy Spirit being the producer of virtue or fruit and the one who

---

6. Jon Amos Comenius, *The Labyrinth of the World and the Paradise of the Heart*, trans. Howard Louthan and Andrea Sterk (Mahwah, NJ: Paulist, 1997) 94.

7. Malcolm Gladwell, *Outliers: The Story of Success* (New York: Little, Brown & Co., 2008).

guides us into wisdom. Yet, God also uses human teachers. In *Talent Is Overrated*, Geoff Colvin, a Senior Editor at Large for *Fortune*, summarizes what scholars of expertise have found to be the ideal interaction between teachers and students. It involves *deliberate practice*, which he describes as "activity designed specifically to improve performance, often with a teacher's help; it can be repeated a lot; feedback on results is continuously available; it's highly demanding mentally . . . and it isn't much fun."[8]

8. Wisdom. Wisdom is neither rule nor virtue, but knowledge that comes from excellent participation in a practice. For instance, as someone who has played point guard in basketball, I acquired knowledge or wisdom about how to make a team work together to score. While you can discover some wisdom on your own, there are again those teachers who have gained wisdom due to their participation, practice, and study (e.g., Solomon). They can provide you the best guidance about how to learn in an area.

9. Models. Models are individuals who incarnate all of the elements mentioned above to achieve excellence in a field. Just as sports or musicians have heroes, every field of learning has its exemplars that are looked to for inspiration.

10. Imagination. Finally, what most of those exemplary models have, as well as others, is the ability to imagine and discover new things in their field of learning. These are the trailblazers and innovators. These are the ones who advance a field of learning and discover new things about the world and its potential that God provided for us. They also see that what may appear to be problems, contradictions, or difficulties may actually be paths to further learning and discovery.

Every university seeks to create advanced learners by inducting students with the necessary knowledge of, or participation in, these elements to some degree. In this respect, Christian universities share a great deal in common with other universities. Yet, there are also obvious differences due to our unique understanding of story and setting.

---

8. Geoff Colvin, *Talent Is Overrated: What Really Separates World-Class Performers from Everybody Else* (New York: Penguin, 2001) 66.

THE FALL OF LEARNING

One of the things that makes Christian universities unique is the explicit recognition that human sinfulness penetrates every area of our lives and the world around us, including our attempts to create excellent learners. Just as in our own lives the Holy Spirit must begin by convicting us of sin, one of the primary tasks of the Christian university should be to demonstrate how this sin deforms learners and learning. Of course, educational institutions may need to confess they are part of the problem. As renowned MIT linguist Noam Chomsky once sarcastically remarked, typically students "come in interested and the process of education is a way of driving that defect out of their minds."[9]

A helpful model of this type of sophisticated Christian critical analysis can be again found in Augustine's *Confessions*, where he divulges the corrupt nature of his early educational life. Augustine realized the whole purpose of his education had fallen aims ("to bring honor among men and to gain deceitful riches"[10]). Yet, his own desires were also fallen as he admitted, "I did not love study and hated to be driven to it, and good was thus done to me, but I myself did not do good. I would have learned nothing unless forced to it,"[11] and confessed what could easily be the confession prayer of many an unmotivated learner, "Yet we sinned by writing, reading, and thinking over our lessons less than was required of us."[12]

His fallen desires stretched from the mental preparation of the classroom to games of physical education. He recalls "Often beaten at games, out of a vain desire for distinction I tried even there for dishonest victories. And what was I so loath to put up with, and what did I so fiercely denounce, if I caught others at it, as what I did to them? If I was caught and argued with, I chose to fight rather than to give in."[13] Augustine realized that his misdirected love deformed every aspect of his being.

Of course, the proper direction of his loves was not helped by the fallen educational system in which he was immersed. The curriculum at school deformed his motivations and emotions by encouraging him to weep for tragic tales about imaginary Greek gods instead of learning to

---

9. Conference titled "Creation & Culture" in Barcelona, Spain, November 25, 1992.

10. Augustine, *Confessions*, trans. John K. Ryan (New York: Penguin, 1961) 51.

11. Ibid., 55.

12. Ibid., 52.

13. Ibid., 62.

weep for his own spiritual death. Moreover, he was taught to despise his bad grammar more than his bad behavior. He recalled, "Thus if a man who accepts or teaches the ancient conventional forms of pronunciation violates the rules of grammar, and utters the word *homo* (man) without sounding the 'h' in the first syllable, he will offend men more than if, contrary to your [God's] law, he who is a man himself would hate another man."[14] It did not help that his teachers also constantly demonstrated their fallen nature. Of one he remembered, "If he was outdone by a fellow teacher in some trifling discussion, he was more tormented by anger and envy than I was when beaten by a playmate in a ball game."[15]

One might easily look down upon a pagan Augustine in his pagan school with pride, but the history of Christian students and educational institutions could include a similar book of confessions about the ways its purposes, curriculum, teachers, and students fell short of high ideals. One could argue some Christian students may be even lazier than non-Christian students because they excuse a lack of learning with spirituality. I myself can remember justifying my lack of pursuit of excellence in academics for spiritual reasons. Christian teachers may also be just as envious or more intellectually sloppy, the curriculum can have similar problems, and priorities can be misplaced (e.g., sports programs over and sometimes against Christian discipleship). They may also too quickly dismiss the insights of pagan or non-Christian scholars without wrestling with the results or the fact that God's common grace may give them tremendous insight. Christians also spend quite a bit of time critiquing the culture perhaps because they have spent so much time in Bible schools and seminaries learning to critique instead of more time in the university learning to create. The need for the redemption of learners requires that we as Christians also confess our shortcomings and transform our whole approach to learning.

THE REDEMPTION OF ADVANCED LEARNERS

Just as the creation of learners is a complicated process, the redemption of learners also proves complex. Although one adopts a different identity, story, and love when converting to Christianity, this adoption does not automatically improve one's learning. The redemption of advanced learning, like any fallen human practice, requires Spirit-filled inspiration and effort

14. Ibid., 61.
15. Ibid., 52.

that works to transform every element involved in its development (story and setting, rules, virtues, practices, models, etc.). Christian universities are created to help with this complex task.

One of fundamental roles of the Christian university is to help students recognize the importance of understanding the implications of competing stories. These alternative narratives will shape the other elements of learning in at least three different ways. First, they will influence the basic terms and interpretive categories used in any discipline. Terms such as "mental and sexual health," "self-actualization and fulfillment," "development," or "public good" cannot be interpreted without implicit assumptions about human well-being that are usually informed by one's guiding narrative.[16] For example, I often ask my class what it means to be morally developed? Can someone with a mental disability, such as the character depicted in the movie *Forrest Gump*, be morally developed? The answer will depend upon whether one understands moral development as merely high-level reasoning skills about moral dilemmas or if one sees moral development as displaying the character of Christ. The understanding from which one proceeds to answer this question often depends upon the larger narrative understanding one uses to shape one's views of the good moral life.

Second, stories guide the language of interpretation. As the Christian psychologists David Myers and Malcolm Jeeves point out, "whether we describe those who favor their own racial and national groups as 'ethnocentric' or as exhibiting strong 'group pride'; whether we view a persuasive message as 'propaganda' or 'education'" will depend upon one's guiding narrative.[17] After all, other nations may view Israel's perception of itself as God's chosen people as "ethnocentric," whereas Christians understand this designation as a special responsibility and blessing bestowed by God.

Third, the presuppositions guiding one's moral interpretations will be also influenced by the themes, feelings, and impulses shaped by one's guiding story. Myers and Jeeves cite as an example the possible different answers to the question, "Is it better to express and act on one's feelings, or to exhibit self-control?"[18] Stories that slant or fail to accurately capture reality or focus only on particular themes that capture partial truths will distort

16. Todd C. Ream and Perry L. Glanzer. *Christian Faith and Scholarship: An Exploration of Contemporary Developments*, ASHE-ERIC Higher Education Report (San Francisco: Jossey-Bass, 2007).

17. David G. Myers and Malcolm A. Jeeves, *Psychology: Through the Eyes of Faith* (New York: Harper, 2003) 14.

18. Ibid., 13.

one's answers to these fundamental questions. For instance, while social class divisions and economic inequities are expressions of the fall, Marxists may reduce the issue to one of economic struggle and propose answers to this problem rooted more in violence than creative sharing and redemptive sacrifice. Similarly, certain biologists or psychologists may explain human behavior by appeals that focus upon the competition of selfish genes without considering other realities. Ultimately, the negative consequences of these reductive stories will need redemption.

Some of these narratives also create both powerful incentives *and* disincentives for learning. Learning may be understood as worthless and a hindrance to a life of pleasure or it may be prized for the money, power, and fame it can provide (as was Augustine's case). Students often need conversion to the proper love of learning—a love inspired by God. When you love someone, you want to learn about them and what they have done. You often ask lots of questions to explore who they are and to learn about their world. Love for God ideally produces in Christians the same burning curiosity about God and God's world. To seek to know about far-flung galaxies, chemical properties and reactions, varieties of fauna, the variety of races, or the intricacies of one's child is to seek to know the one we love. Abandoning one's love for a life filled with various endless diversions appears quite inconsistent with any profession of love. In contrast, Christian students and universities should be known for their intellectual passion, curiosity, and vigor.

This transformation will influence more than the larger story and setting. Consider the rules of learning and the reasons for obeying them. For example, my secular undergraduate university had an honor code that enforced the rules of learning. The notion of "honor" and "honor codes" at this institution derived largely from a Southern culture that prized social reputation. While the cultural pressures of Southern honor may prove compelling for some, it remains geographically and metaphysically limited. In my own experience, I did not cheat on Professor Garside's take-home history test, despite my lack of preparation and knowledge, to uphold some sense of Southern honor. I was not a Southerner or from a wealthy family—the idea of losing my honor had little power and meaning in those contexts. I was a Christian and that tradition energized my moral will so I would not compromise my integrity for a possible A or B on the test (full confession time—I received a C+). You have to own a moral tradition and its virtues and be convinced by the persuasiveness of its story and its moral exemplars in order for it to truly take hold. Why even stick to obeying the rules and having integrity? Yes, God says so, but there are reasons behind the command. Living honestly is how one becomes fully human and bears the image of God. It is the secret to life. In fact, the whole pursuit of wisdom to which we are commanded (e.g., Proverbs 4) involves acquiring the way to life that God established at the foundation of the world.

A Christian university will recognize the importance of certain kinds of virtue for learning. In his book *Exiles from Eden: Religion and the Academic Vocation in America*,[19] Valparaiso University's provost Mark Schwehn argues the *ethos* of the modern university has been corrupted by modern approaches to the academic vocation that separate intellectual and moral virtue from the transmission of knowledge and skills and the making of knowledge. In contrast, he argues the Christian virtues of humility, faith, self-sacrifice, and charity are essential for the communal quest for knowledge and truth. Certainly, the ideal Christian university would cultivate learners who can apply these virtues to their fields of study, as well as to other areas of their lives.

These types of virtues require special forms of practice along with God's grace. The redemption of learning practices involves making sure we train our body in every dimension of life, particularly when it comes to our devotion to God. Our commitment to Christ only amplifies this need and provides added motivation. As the apostle Paul wrote in 1 Corinthians 9:25, "Everyone who competes in the games goes into strict training. They do it to get a crown that will not last; but we do it to get a crown that will last forever. Therefore . . . I beat my body and make it my slave so that after I have preached to others I myself will not be disqualified for the prize." Christian discipleship involves placing our bodies under Christ's lordship. The redemption of learning practices will involve integrating the practices found in the Christian community and church, such as hospitality, enacting charity with texts, keeping time differently, and more.[20]

All of these elements work together in the creation of individuals with a unique imagination for advanced learning. Former Columbia University educational philosopher Douglas Sloan makes the argument that since knowledge is participatory, the quality of knowledge we acquire about the

---

19. Mark Schwehn, *Exiles from Eden: Religion and the Academic Vocation in America* (New York: Oxford, 1993).

20. David I. Smith and James K. A. Smith, *Teaching and Christian Practices: Reshaping Faith and Learning* (Grand Rapids: Eerdmans, 2011).

world will depend upon "the quality of the participants and the quality of their participation." In other words:

> The possibility of a deepening of knowledge, thus, presupposes a constant working on oneself, on the full development of thinking, feeling, willing and character as essential to the fullness of cognition. The basic religious attitudes, for example, of wonder and reverence as readiness for what the other has to reveal, can, thereby, become more than mere inner feeling states. They can become primary cognitive organs without which nothing of genuine newness can be known.[21]

If Sloan is correct, the particular virtues or character qualities that Christianity cultivates also become distinct tools for knowing and intellectual imagination.

THE CREATION AND REDEMPTION OF ADVANCED LEARNING

While both Christian colleges and universities focus upon creating learners, what generally sets a university apart from a college is that full-time professors are expected to engage in creative scholarly projects within their respective fields. They create art, music, or screenplays. They write books, compose sonnets, and create new ways of understanding society, the human body, nature, and more. For Christians, creating learning means producing culture that enhances our love of God, furthers human flourishing, gives insight into God's creation, or produces new cultural creations using the latent capacities within God's creation.

One actually finds that these theological realities helped produce the first universities. Historian Walter Rüegg provides a list of distinctive ideas originating from Christian theology that nourished the desire to learn and know in the Middle Ages and culminated in the creation of the first European universities.

- The belief in a world order, created by God, rational, accessible to human reason, to be explained by human reason and to be mastered by it; this belief underlies scientific and scholarly research as the attempt to understand this rational order of God's creation.

---

21. Douglas Sloan, *Faith and Knowledge: Mainline Protestantism and American Higher Education* (Louisville, KY: Westminster John Knox, 1994) 236.

- Respect for the individual as a reflection of the macrocosm or as having been formed in the image of God laid the foundation for the gradually realized freedom of scientific and scholarly research and teaching.

- The recognition of scientific and scholarly knowledge as a public good that is ultimately a gift of God resulted in less interest within the universities in the economic use of scientific knowledge than there had been in the learned professions outside the university.

- The equality of human beings, which is part of natural law, first found an institutional arrangement for scientific and scholarly study in the setting provided by the university.[22]

Of course, secular universities today engage in the creation of learning even without this theological narrative, and in fact these universities currently produce the bulk of new discoveries about the world. The job of the Christian university, however, is to continue to nourish the creation of learning within the fertile theological soil that first gave birth to universities.

Being involved in the creation of learning ideally helps a teacher create learning in students. Expert practitioners in their respective fields possess the wisdom of what contributes to that expertise that others who merely teach about a field but do not practice it will not achieve. This practical striving for excellence can then be passed along to students. Ironically, some students and parents argue that they want to attend an institution of higher education where professors are not "distracted" by their own research (which they often consider to be of dubious value). In this respect, they show little appreciation for the creation of learning. It would be like saying I do not want a practicing basketball player to teach my son or daughter basketball, because he or she is too distracted by learning to be a good basketball player. The Christian university should be a place where professors are seeking excellence in the creation of learning in all of their respective fields and thus also introduce their students to these critical practices.

Of course, as sinful human beings, the learning that we create will always be marred by the fall (which will be true for all universities). Consequently, all learning must constantly be redeemed—some forms of learning more so than others. For example, an analysis of why a school or educational system is failing by a scholar may be quite complex in its analysis, but

---

22. Walter Rüegg, "Themes," in *A History of the University in Europe: Vol. 1, Universities in the Middle Ages*, ed. Hilde de Ridder-Symoens (Cambridge: Cambridge University Press, 1992) 32–33.

it still may fail to miss a few key factors. Still, a shoddy analysis may fail to capture both the complexity of the problems and many key factors leading to the school or system's failure.

Of course, Christ accomplished the ultimate redemption by restoring God's reign (the kingdom of God) but we are also asked to join in that work (i.e., freeing God's creation as well as human creations from the bondage of the fall). Particularly in the area of redeeming human learning, Christian universities have a special understanding of this unique calling. Yet, it is important to realize that through common grace, anyone can be and is involved in advancing redemptive forms of learning that free aspects of God's creation from some effects of the fall.

For example, the historian who creates a masterful biography of an historical figure that corrects an unjust critique of that figure is also involved in both the creation and redemption of scholarship. Scientists who help discover cures for disease or gain greater insight into how to reverse human damage to the environment are involved in this project. New insights into God's creation that create technology also create new opportunities for corruption (e.g., internet pornography and extortion schemes). Thus, Christians, following the example of the triune God, must create new ways to reverse the sinful effects of our own creations (e.g., critiquing unjust laws that create oppressive economic or political systems, researching institutions or corporate structures and revealing possible ways they may dehumanize others, discovering ways to restore an environment damaged by human abuse, etc.).

We must also remember that, in the end, the ever-present danger of our fallen nature is to see in these new discoveries and arrangements our final hope (e.g., the new technological savior or socialist utopia). We become the ones in control of the creation and redemption instead of co-participants with the one who ultimately creates and redeems all learners and learning. It is this final idolatrous temptation which is the bane of all those involved in higher learning. We forget that scholars also need redemption. By God's grace, we do not put our hopes in new human creations, but in the one who has allowed and inspired such creation and who accomplishes our redemption.

QUESTIONS FOR DISCUSSION

1. What is the difference between the "integration of faith and learning" and "the creation and redemption of learners and learning"?

2. Of the ten areas listed that relate to becoming a learner, which one do you find the most difficult in understanding? Living?

3. How does the Christian story and understanding of reality influence your approach to learning?

4. What particular virtues do professors seek to have students practice?

5. In what ways are you involved in the creation of learning?

6. What would the redemption of learning look like in your particular field?

Chapter Five

Joining Our Work with God's Work

The meaning of work is not a function
of management theory or salesmanship.[1]

—Arthur F. Holmes, *The Idea of a Christian College*

I STILL REMEMBER THAT disturbing thought process. While pondering an overwhelming array of occupational options during my senior year in high school, I eliminated the alternatives with a simple question: What career will fit my interests, provide long-term job security, and produce a high salary? I decided upon engineering for the simple reason that there were numerous job openings promising large salaries. Only a year later, I would look back on my choice with regret.

In retrospect, I have often wondered why salary and security guided my initial decision about a college major. I took my Christian faith seriously in many other major decisions, yet I made one of life's most important choices without the trace of a Christian mind. Later, I learned I was not alone. Princeton University sociologist Robert Wuthnow has discovered a similar approach to most career choices: "Asked if their religious beliefs had influenced their choice of their career, most of the people I interviewed in recent years, Christians and non-Christians alike, said no. Asked if they thought of their work as a calling, most said no. Asked if they understood

1. Arthur Holmes, *The Idea of a Christian College* (Grand Rapids: Eerdmans, 1987) 39.

the concept of stewardship, most said no. Asked how religion did influence their work lives or thoughts about money, most said the two were completely separate."[2] What accounts for this phenomenon?

Education may play a role. The secular university I attended did little to help me think through the relationship between my future career and my overall philosophy of life. The Christian educational tradition in which I was raised also failed me at this point. It used words such as "calling" or "vocation" only with regard to full-time forms of ministry, but it did not do the same with other so-called "secular" jobs. While the Christian parachurch community in which I participated often supplemented what I missed at a secular university and church with regard to Christian formation, in this case it also proved deficient. The basic mindset the group instilled was that I should invest in eternal things—which meant evangelism and discipleship (and discipleship did not involve my course of study). In this view, university education became a secondary concern to and even a distraction from the true calling to make disciples. Our majors and future careers were conceived of as something that should support ministry, but they were not considered expressions of our faith.

Such a mentality proves problematic if we consider that most students will not join an overtly Christian ministry. Furthermore, we will likely spend over two-fifths of our waking lives at work.[3] The Christian university must set before students a grand vision of the Christian narrative that encompasses all of life. For if students are shuffled into career or professional placement counseling that mimics the same language and operates from the same paradigm as secular universities, the Christian university has failed. Furthermore, merely justifying the career benefits of a liberal arts education will not always be applicable in the setting of a comprehensive university. A creative and redemptive Christian university must be different.

---

2. Robert Wuthnow, *Christianity in the 21st Century* (New York: Oxford University Press, 1993) 200.

3. Lisa Belkin, "Time Wasted? Perhaps It's Well Spent," *The New York Times* (May 31, 2007) www.nytimes.com/2007/05/31/fashion/31work.html?spc=19&sq=&st=nty.

CREATION AND WORK:
STEWARDSHIP, VOCATION, AND CALLING

One of the most important things a Christian university should do is introduce students to the ways our different loves alter how we approach work. Unfortunately, it is not often clear in the curricular or cocurricular lives of most Christian universities where such connections are made. I would suggest that such conversations should occur in a first-year seminar or the introductory courses of every major and should include placing work in the context of the Christian story.

This story of work starts with creation. As human beings made in the image of God, we work because God works. Of course, we work differently and the identity God imparted to us makes this clear. One of the identities God bestowed upon us during creation and emphasized again by Christ concerns that of being a steward, manager, or ruler (Gen 1:26; Matt 21:33–40; 25:14–30; Luke 16:1–13; 17:7–9). Stewardship involves managing God's creations (e.g., nature, animals, humans—including our own body) and human creations (such as money and other forms of human culture). One way humans have drawn upon and expanded the potential found in God's creation is by creating specific professions that steward a particular aspect of God's creation. We sometimes call such God-ordained professions "vocations." For example, we created the vocations of architecture, biology, chemistry, computer science, engineering, graphic design, mathematics, music, physics, teaching, theater, and more.

As a student, I often understood the terms "vocation" and "calling" as the same thing. However, it is best to distinguish between the two. A vocation, as described above, is a profession created to steward part of God's good creation. A calling should be understood as what God, through gifting, circumstances, special summons, and other forms of grace, gives to someone who responds by taking upon him or herself a particular identity role and vocation. One could think of the prophets or the disciples. Oddly, one will sometimes find the term "calling" being used in a nontheistic context, although there is actually no one doing the calling unless one considers hearing from oneself as a calling—which is an odd and tragic replacement for God.

Based on biblical examples, some Christian communities such as those I experienced associate calling with vocations linked to full-time Christian service such as pastors, missionaries, and staff members of Christian organizations. This mindset dates back to the medieval Catholic Church. According to this view, receiving a sacred calling from God involved being called to the specific vocation of monastic or church life. The sixteenth-century Protestant reformers, Martin Luther and John Calvin, criticized this limitation of God's calling to only spiritual vocations. They argued that one could be called to "worldly" vocations and such callings and vocations could be undertaken for God's glory and kingdom. Furthermore, they argued that roles beyond one's particular occupation, such as being a mother or father, a citizen, and more, also should be considered vocations. While I agree with the Reformers regarding this last point, the scope of this chapter can unfortunately only focus specifically on occupational vocations.

THE ROLE OF THE UNIVERSITY

We have created educational institutions and particularly universities to be the major cultural institutions that both initiate young people into certain occupational vocations and study these vocations to improve the practice within them. For instance, a business school in a university seeks to teach accounting majors to master a particular human business practice and to study how to improve that practice. Furthermore, professors at universities, even more so than colleges, engage in teaching graduate students how to steward a particular discipline at an advanced level. The first doctoral degree was awarded in the United States in 1861 and today more than 40,000 doctoral degrees are awarded every year. As one scholar of graduate studies wrote, "The Ph.D. is expected to serve as a steward of her discipline or profession, dedicated to the integrity of its work in the generation, critique, transformation, transmission, and use of knowledge."[4] Notice the biblical language used to describe the responsibility of the graduate program. In this respect, universities are increasingly participants in the creation and sustaining of this unique form of stewardship that can serve God and others.

Every vocation has some generally agreed-upon standards of excellence or what it would mean to be a good [fill in the vocational blank]. Historians, accountants, and biologists all seek to initiate students into the knowledge base and practices necessary to be a good practitioner in those

4. Lee S. Schulman as quoted in Chris M. Golde, "Preparing Stewards of the Discipline," in *Envisioning the Future of Doctoral Education: Preparing Stewards of the Discipline, Carnegie Essays on the Doctorate*, eds. Chris M. Golde, George E. Walker, and associates (San Francisco: Jossey-Bass, 2006) 3.

particular fields. In addition, as outlined in the last chapter, there are particular ways we initiate a novice into the practices associated with a field of learning. All of this could be said to be humanity's way of being good stewards of God's creation. We've learned to expand upon and create whole new areas of knowledge and practice from the resources God gave us. Of course, secularists do not conceive of their task in this way, but they also set forth visions of what it would mean to be excellent in particular fields of study. To be good in any vocation, to be a steward of one's area of calling, involves giving attention to the following elements of vocational formation that were discussed in the previous chapter.

1. Placing One's Vocation in the Bigger Story

Every professional mentor embeds his or her vocation into a larger story and setting for matters of motivation or accountability. Professors in a school of education may remind future teachers that they shape future generations. We need scientists, science professors may suggest, to help our nation advance technologically. The ancient Hippocratic Oath (fifth century B.C.) sworn by doctors begins, "I swear by Apollo, Physician, by Asclepius, by Hygieia, by Panacea, and all the gods and goddesses, making them my witnesses that I will carry out according to my ability and judgment this oath . . ."[5]

While Christians may acknowledge some of these stories and settings and reject others, a Christian university also sets before students a unique guiding story of a particular vocation in at least two ways. First, a Christian university will emphasize that one's primary motivation stems not only from a concern for serving others, the common good, or the good of a particular group (e.g., citizens, shareholders) all of which secular universities will usually emphasize, but it will stem primarily from a sense of accountability to the One whose creation we are stewarding. When Jesus tells a parable about a steward, the steward is not primarily working for his fellow stewards or even the common good, but for the master. Second, numerous practical implications will flow from this perspective. One can take joy in cocreating with God (which requires a degree of dependence) one can learn to draw boundaries against workaholism (our true "boss" has ordered us to rest) and misguided loyalties to companies, institutions, or even the professional society supposedly nurturing the health of the vocation must be resisted.

5. Hippocrates, *Hippocrates*, vol. 1, trans. W. H. S. Jones (Cambridge, MA: Harvard University Press, 1948) 299.

2. The Role of the Liberal Arts

A Christian university will continue to prize the relationship between the liberal arts and one's vocation. Since it values placing everything in a larger story, it will place a vocation in the context of theology, history, sociology, and other disciplines. It will attempt to help students see God's role in the story of this vocation and the humanness of the vocation—the wondrous creative role it plays, its limits in light of the larger human story and realm of knowledge, and its potential with the body of humanity for good. Without such a perspective, the university becomes little more than a technical school in that it focuses upon practical job skills and is reduced, in the phrase of one philosopher, to "the barbarism of specialization."[6]

Any scientific vocation provides a good example. Good science students usually learn how to employ the scientific method and particular analytical tools to study a distinct aspect of nature. This method, created and honed by scientists, has obviously shown great potential for unlocking the secrets and mysteries of God's world. Yet, students must also be taught to think critically about science, the scientific method, and the results of its discoveries (e.g., unlocking the secrets of the atom to create the atomic bomb). To do so, it helps to view science from the perspective of other disciplines in the liberal arts (theology, philosophy, history, and sociology). Noted historian of science Thomas Kuhn once argued that, unfortunately, the education of scientists is often "a narrow and rigid education" that rarely involves undertaking a liberal education about how to think critically about science.[7] Warren Nord, an educational philosopher who served on the faculty at the University of North Carolina, Chapel Hill, even noted, "The education of scientists is much narrower when it comes to religion, than that of clergy or theologians when it comes to science."[8] The Christian scientist educated at a Christian university should be different in this respect.

3. & 4. The Ends and Rules of the Vocation

Every vocation will also have an implicit or explicit purpose and a set of rules. The ancient Hippocratic Oath for doctors mentioned earlier states,

6. José Ortega Y Gasset, *The Revolt of the Masses* (Notre Dame, IN: University of Notre Dame Press, 1985) 94–100.

7. Thomas Kuhn, *The Structure of Scientific Revolutions* (Chicago: University of Chicago Press, 1962) 165.

8. Warren Nord, *Does God Make a Difference? Taking Religion Seriously in Our Schools and Universities* (New York: Oxford University Press, 2010) 244.

"I will use treatment to help the sick according to my ability and judgment, but never with a view to injury and wrong-doing . . . I will not give to a woman a pessary to cause abortion. But I will keep pure and holy both my life and my art."[9] Modern vocations have more recent professional codes of ethics or rules and interestingly, they are much more vocationally narrow. The source of these rules is the reason and experience of particular professional associations.

Christian universities provide a metanarrative by which students can learn how to critically analyze these ends and rules. For instance, here's a professional rule from the Information Systems Audit and Control Association: "Maintain the privacy and confidentiality of information obtained in the course of their activities unless disclosure is required by legal authority. Such information shall not be used for personal benefit or released to inappropriate parties."[10] In this case, the code merely specifies one of the Ten Commandments ("Do not steal") in the context of the profession. While not clearly stated, all vocational rules assume some sort of moral order. While one might hear about relativism throughout a secular university, in reality, every professor introducing students in a vocation is a moralist. Of course, rules always raise lots of questions. The most important question is always, "Why?" Here is where one's larger belief system plays an important role. Christians believe God established a moral order from which we derive these types of rules.

Furthermore, the Christian narrative may help one raise critical questions about these rules. For example, part of the code of ethics from the National Association of Social Workers, "Social workers should act to prevent and eliminate domination of, exploitation of, and discrimination against any person, group, or class on the basis of race, ethnicity, national origin, color, sex, sexual orientation, gender identity or expression, age, marital status, political belief, religion, immigration status, or mental or physical disability."[11] While Christians would likely agree with a substantial portion of this code, the code raises many questions. Should a social worker fight to eliminate the Catholic Church's practice of only ordaining single, male priests? Obviously, in this case, one's identity and associated ethics as a Christian and a social worker may clash and one will have to choose which one is more important.

9. Hippocrates, *Hippocrates*, 299.

10. http://www.isaca.org/Certification/Code-of-Professional-Ethics/Pages/default.aspx

11. http://www.socialworkers.org/pubs/code/code.asp

5. & 6. Virtues and Practice for the Vocation

While Christians are called to exercise the whole range of the fruits of the Spirit or Christian virtue, particular vocations will require the development of these virtues in ways that may be unique to the discipline. For example, an elementary school teacher and an entrepreneur develop different types of patience and creativity. An accountant and a doctor will need to learn what it means to practice truthfulness in their unique professional context. Unfortunately, we sometimes assume that since we have learned to practice a virtue in one context, we will easily be able to transfer the practice of that virtue to another context.

The reality, however, is much different. *The New York Times* columnist David Brooks helpfully summarizes the matter, "Students who are routinely dishonest at home are not routinely dishonest at school. People who are courageous at work can be cowardly at church. People who behave kindly on a sunny day may behave callously the next day when it is cloudy and they are feeling glum. Behavior does not exhibit what the psychologists call 'cross-situational stability.'"[12] In other words, just like hitting a ball is different in baseball, racquetball, and tennis, learning patience is different for me as a professional, husband, father, and a citizen (particularly when driving on the freeway). The virtues are specific to the vocation and thus require specific forms of deliberate practice as described in the last chapter.

7. & 8. Mentors and Wisdom

Wisdom comes from an excellent pursuit of the goods of a vocation while pursuing those goods within its rules and using the necessary virtues. As a point guard in basketball, I know from experience that players take the most high-percentage three-point shots when I drive in the lane and kick out an accurate pass from the lane instead of making a pass from the top of the key to the side (as you see, the person with wisdom usually knows the technical language required to describe excellence). In a vocation, such wisdom comes from those who have been excellent in a field—usually what we would call mentors and models.

Universities, as stewards of the disciplines, ideally include professors who attempt to discover, articulate, and expand this vocational wisdom. This is why graduate studies are a vital part of the calling of a Christian

---

12. David Brooks, "Where the Wild Things Are," *The New York Times* (October 20, 2009) A31.

university. Undertaking advanced study with a mentor in the field is where such wisdom is most likely to be discovered, articulated, and expanded. From the student's vantage point, that is also why faculty members at a Christian university must also be actively engaged in the active discovery and dissemination of knowledge.

9. & 10. Models and Imagination

Every vocational field has great practitioners. Finding those mentors at the Christian university would be the ideal. The reality is that Christians may not always be the best in their field. What a Christian university should provide, however, are those who are the best at thinking about and teaching others how to be the best at being a Christian in a particular field. If not, students will need to encounter examples in other settings or through books about how to incarnate what it means to be a good Christian in a specific field and the type of imagination it takes.

FALLEN VOCATIONS

Given that humans are fallen, every occupational vocation in which one will enter is also fallen. One job of the Christian university is to educate students about the complexity of the fall and how it touches every aspect of a discipline or profession including its unique tools and subject matter, the professors engaged with it, the students learning it, and those practicing it. Students have developed a fine capacity for identifying the general vices of adults, their fellow students, and perhaps even themselves, but they may not recognize the subtle sins in a professional field.

Take the sciences or social sciences for example. One of the prideful views sometimes found in these fields is the assumption that one can achieve human flourishing only using a limited range of intellectual tools. In this case, the scientific method, which has clearly been an amazingly successful learning tool, may become the only tool suggested by which one can build the house of human flourishing. While human creativity exhibited through technology proves wondrous, it also becomes the object of our faith and hope since it appears to offer solutions to so many human problems. In other words, it becomes an idol. Of course, anyone who has sent an e-mail or a text message he or she regretted also realizes it enhances and magnifies his or her sinfulness in other ways. Part of developing critical thinking in the Christian university is to make students aware of the limits of the various disciplinary tools provided by the university.

Consider the *Diagnostic and Statistical Manual of Mental Disorders* (DSM), the primary handbook of psychiatric diagnosis. Recently Allen Frances, the former chairman of the psychiatry department at Duke University School of Medicine, led the task force that produced the fourth version of the DSM and wrote about possible changes to the fifth volume. He expressed concern that this "Bible of psychiatry's"[13] boundary of mental illness would be changed so that tens of millions of people we would consider normal today would suddenly be classified as mentally ill. Despite his heavy involvement in creating the third and fourth editions, he suggested that the American Psychological Association "should lose its century-old monopoly on defining mental illness." He claimed the new version "will introduce many new and unproven diagnoses that will medicalize normality and result in a glut of unnecessary and harmful drug prescription[s]."[14] These mistakes, he argued, are "the result of an intellectual conflict of interest; experts always overvalue their pet area and want to expand its purview, until the point that everyday problems come to be mislabeled as mental disorders. Arrogance, secretiveness, passive governance, and administrative disorganization have also played a role."[15]

While this example comes from psychology, examples could be gathered from every field. Sin pervades every discipline and Christians in any vocation must be equipped to identify how vice may undermine the discipline and how to move forward in a redemptive manner in order to reverse the effects of the fall in a vocation.

REDEMPTION AND RESTORATION

Vocations need direction. I recently attended a lecture where an award-winning professor described the purpose of university education as simply changing the lives of students. The problem is that sometimes professors can change students' lives for the worse and vocations can be used for evil ends. Change, in and of itself, is not a good. Christians seek to engage in the kind of change God initiated on earth. God's redemptive activity, as mentioned in Colossians 1:20, involves God in Christ reconciling "to

13. Allen Frances, "Diagnosing the D.S.M.," *The New York Times* (May 12, 2012) A19.

14. Ibid.

15. Ibid.

himself all things, whether things on earth or things in heaven." The triune God invites us to join in the creative development of the potential found in God's university and the redemption of all creation. Christians, the church, and the Christian university have the tremendous opportunity to live out what an acceptance of that invitation entails with regard to professional vocations. Being a steward of a vocation now involves joining with Christ in Spirit-guided and empowered efforts to reverse the effects of the fall in that specific dimension of life.

What does redemption involve in a particular vocation? Occasionally, the answers are quite clear and one hardly needs a university education to figure it out. Yet, quite often, the problems are incredibly complex and the way to think about the issue in light of the Christian tradition is difficult to ascertain. In these areas, the Christian university proves essential in helping Christians and the church address issues. Ideally, Christian university faculty mentor their students and help them understand what loving God looks like when engaged in a particular discipline. For example, Christian historians should be able to provide young historians with wisdom about how to conduct research, interact with sources, charitably interpret opposing views, and truly love their subject. What this might mean for writing a biography of a historical figure requires tremendous wisdom. Does the figure need to be rehabilitated from unfair interpretations and characterizations? How does one choose to tell the story of a person who perhaps demonstrates a mix of tremendous virtues but also serious vices and flaws? Historians who are Christians may have a wide range of opinions.

Moreover, Christians do not always agree. Consider what the redemption of the practice of psychology might look like. For instance, a recent book about how best to integrate Christianity and psychology identified five different types of approaches Christians have suggested.[16] The idea that there is one particular way to be a Christian nurse, author, accountant, psychologist, etc., must be recognized as problematic in any complex vocational practice. Loving God or God's creation in any context often proves the subject of considerable discussion and disagreement. The complexity of the issues will require lifelong conversations with other Christian professionals. One of the best ways to continue one's discipleship in this area even beyond university life is to become involved in a Christian professional

16. Eric L. Johnson, ed., *Psychology and Christianity: Five Views*, 2nd ed. (Downers Grove, IL: InterVarsity, 2010).

society related to one's profession.[17] Within the context of these societies, one can undertake the technical discussion necessary regarding both theology and one's particular field of learning. He or she can also think through various creative and redemptive approaches to problems in his or her field.

One of my relatives can testify to both the tragedy of fallen vocation and creative and redemptive glory of that same vocation. Born with an attached spinal cord, which today is fortunately often caught at a young age, Rod was misdiagnosed as having a slipped disk at age sixteen. Even worse, the dye he was given to perform a myelogram to determine the problem caused an allergic reaction. This dye was later taken off the market after its possible destructive consequences were realized—consequences the company that made it, according to records, appeared to try and cover up. The end result was that the lining of his spinal cord was burned, creating a condition called Arachnoiditis. The result was tragic. Rod, who is married with two young girls and held a job as an academic dean in a university, was forced to spend most of his life in bed living with pain that on a one to ten scale he describes as level nine or ten, all the while on tremendous amounts of painkillers. For significant periods of time, he could not even get out of the house to see his daughters' school events and activities or attend church.

Yet, human creativity that would reverse the effects of these tragic consequences of sinful humanity has brought new relief for Rod. Due to the development of a new type of spinal cord stimulator that is now available in Europe, which Rod had placed in his back, he now is experiencing a brand-new level of relief from his pain, which at times he says is only at level two. He was able to attend his oldest daughter's graduation, can walk the dogs around the block, drive and enjoy longer periods of time in human society, from which he often felt isolated. All of this happened due to a team of people—inventors, doctors, and others—who used their vocations to create and implement something new that might alleviate human suffering. They not only practiced stewardship of their talents and gifts and received mentorship, but they also engaged in the imaginative and redemptive work of envisioning new ways to relieve the pain we find in our fallen world.

Still, Rod experiences the psychological, spiritual, and physical scars of pain. The effects of the fall are still with him and continue to shape who

---

17. For a list of Christian professional societies, see Todd C. Ream and Perry L. Glanzer, *Christian Faith and Scholarship: An Exploration of Contemporary Developments* (San Francisco: Jossey-Bass, 2007) 80–81.

he is. Ultimately, we know that even the redemptive work of the individuals in these vocations is only a provisional one. Only with the final restoration of God's kingdom by Christ will there actually be no more pain. While we seek to join God in his creative and redemptive work, we also must wait for God's final work to fulfill the ultimate restoration of the kingdom.

QUESTIONS FOR DISCUSSION

1. What is a calling? What is a vocation? What is the difference between the two?

2. Why did you choose your particular career or major? How did you conceive of the career and the process when making your decision?

3. How have you heard vocations placed in a larger story and setting? What are the assumed purposes when making this placement?

4. What virtues are necessary for your vocation? What vices do you have to avoid? Do you think there is anything specifically Christian about your understanding of them or your thoughts about how they are acquired?

5. Who are the best mentors and models in your field? What makes them the best?

6. How do you see your vocation as fallen and in need of redemption?

Chapter Six

Practicing the Academic Vocation

There is no room here for a dichotomy between what is secular and what is sacred, for everything about people created in God's image belongs to God—that is, it is sacred.[1]

—Arthur F. Holmes, *The Idea of a Christian College*

Jacob was an impressive student with a set of God-given abilities allowing him to choose from a wide variety of vocations in life. He had a keen analytical mind. He spoke well and his writing skills were at the top of his class. Due to his deep Christian faith, he had chosen to attend a Christian university so that he could meet Christian friends and continue to cultivate his faith (ideally, he also wanted to meet a young woman who shared his faith commitments).

While at the university, he settled on majoring in finance and minoring in economics. The campus had strong faculty members in those fields and Jacob thought he would be well prepared to enter the business field and well positioned to earn an MBA when the time was right. In addition, he thought studying with these faculty members might also help him develop a deeper understanding of the importance of ethical practices in the business world.

Jacob did well in the classroom. He had a wide circle of great friends. He was active in student government and was highly sought after for

1. Arthur Holmes, *The Idea of a Christian College* (Grand Rapids: Eerdmans, 1987) 16.

intramural teams (he even met a young woman he would eventually marry). However, he had not anticipated that the demands of learning would combine his identity as a Christian with his vocation as a finance major. Professors routinely contended that one's faith in Christ was the foundation for all other forms of understanding and that theological commitments provided the frameworks for how practices in finance and theories in economics were understood. Jacob's professors consistently challenged the notions that financial markets were neutral and that certain dimensions of our lives were inappropriate for economic exchange. Professors who embodied faith-seeking understanding set before him a new understanding of what it means to love God.

Despite Jacob's impressive academic preparation, however, his prior Christian formation set him up for a problem. The Christian community in which he had grown up had left him with the understanding that religion was primarily an emotional enterprise and that one's connection to God was most pronounced through sincere waves of feeling. Moments when he perceived he was closest to God were moments when God's presence prompted emotions such as joy and comfort. What he had not learned was how to love God in other dimensions of life.

A study-abroad trip to central Africa became the context for Jacob to suddenly experience how he might also love God in the context of his vocation. While traveling through village after village without access to adequate drinking water, his heart went out to the people living in them. His mind was asking what conditions led to the oppression they were facing. His body was overwhelmed by the heat and the lack of access to a critical resource needed to sustain life. Ultimately, his spirit cried out with questions he was not yet prepared to answer. Jacob then asked himself whether God was calling him to do anything. He could not deny God was moving in his life in ways he may not have otherwise perceived.

After graduation, Jacob took a job working as an economic development officer for a nearby community. While he thrived in his work, he was not able to shake his experiences in central Africa. As time moved along, he persuaded other members of the church to use their collective resources to devise strategies to support families needing access to suitable water. They asked not only what could be done in the short term to provide the individuals living in these African villages with suitable drinking water but what also needed to be done in the long term to remove any systemic barriers that might be in place. Eventually, they formed a non-profit organization that sought to not only drill wells in places that desperately needed them but to also train and employ local villagers to drill and maintain the wells, as they wanted to provide resources to people on the ground who could carry out this work for generations to come.

Jacob's story is not unique. Many students arrive on Christian university campuses with the understanding that the church should be a place that cultivates our emotional and/or spiritual well-being but that Christianity has little to do with our intellectual or physical well-being, especially if our majors are not in Christian ministry. Loving God and our neighbors makes demands on all of our identity. Augustine and many of his successors spoke of faith seeking understanding. Faith proved to be the basis for their means of exploring and appreciating God's world. However, as the university secularized, religion later became a narrowly understood experience connected only with our emotional well-being.

The worship of God through our calling is not limited to one or two dimensions of our identity. In contrast, God demands our all—our heart, our soul, and our mind. No one single dimension is left behind in our pursuit of loving God and our neighbor. Our bodies are not baptized apart from our minds. Our minds are not baptized apart from our hearts. In our efforts to live out the charge given to us upon our baptism, no portion of who we are is allowed to be left behind as we seek to love God and our neighbor.

As both Jacob and Augustine learned, God does not make demands on one dimension of our identity. Instead, all of who we are is called upon to be placed under the lordship of Jesus Christ. The church then calls upon the Christian university to play a critical role in advancing its mission to the world—a mission that includes an integrated understanding of what it means to be human and the diverse array of callings human beings are challenged to live out in this world.

One of the ways those in a Christian university can best learn about this process is to get to know Christian scholars who attempt a more holistic approach to learning and life. We need models in our practices who can give us an idea of what this might look like within the university. What follows is thus a brief introduction to several Christians practicing or who practiced the academic vocation, who wrestled with this challenge, and who also made considerable contributions to how Christians in the university can understand their calling.

MARK A. NOLL—A CHRISTIAN HISTORIAN

Mark Noll served the majority of his teaching career at his undergraduate alma mater, Wheaton College, but now serves on the faculty at the University of Notre Dame. As a practicing historian, Noll finds it difficult when Christians fail to connect their faith to learning and secular historians ignore the presence of faith in the lives of the individuals and organizations they study. These Christians fail to appreciate the past and its contributions to an array of present challenges. Compounding this problem is the way the field of history has rarely considered religion to be a critical component of understanding the past. If religion is simply an emotional experience relegated to what is deemed our private lives, that logic makes sense. However, as a historian Noll believes the Christian faith is largely based upon events from the past, and most notably, the life of Christ.

Much of what Noll argues then is that religion makes larger claims on what it means to be human and thus is often central to understanding the past for both Christians and secularists. For example, in *America's God: From Jonathan Edwards to Abraham Lincoln*, Noll argues that in order to understand a critical portion of America's past, one must also understand the religious convictions present at that time. Contrary to the prevailing wisdom that evangelicalism is a relatively recent invention and defined by a reactionary compulsion to the wider culture, Noll contends, "For the period under consideration the most widely recognized religious voices for the American public were Protestant. From the 1790s and with gathering force in the decades leading to the Civil War, the most prominent Protestant voices were also self-consciously evangelical."[2] In many ways, Christianity was a vital part of the decisions being made at critical junctures in the nation's history and many of those individuals were evangelicals.

In perhaps what is his most widely recognized book, *The Scandal of the Evangelical Mind*, Noll chronicles how evangelicals failed to uphold a high view of the academic vocation and thus failed to maintain leadership in American academic life. He not only indicts the present generation of evangelicals for their lack of scholarly productivity but also points to ill-conceived forms of history as contributing to this dilemma. His work opens with the assertion, "This book is an epistle from a wounded lover. As one who is in love with the life of the mind but who has also been drawn to

---

2. Mark A. Noll, *America's God: From Jonathan Edwards to Abraham Lincoln* (New York: Oxford University Press, 2002) 5.

faith in Christ through the love of evangelical Protestants."[3] While these two loves are generally perceived to be irreconcilable in the present, Noll believes an accurate reading of history proves that was not entirely true in the past. While key theological movements contributed to this dilemma, Noll believes "the greatest hope for evangelical thought lies with the heart of the evangelical message concerning the cross of Christ."[4] In one of his more recent books, *Jesus Christ and the Life of the Mind*, Noll then expands upon this assertion and offers a more systematic appraisal of what is at stake when the cross of Christ is placed at the center of scholarly practices.

An illustration of what this might mean for his vocation can be found in the way that Noll believes Christianity aids his historical inquiries. In his essay, "Teaching History as a Christian," he describes how he believes Christianity gives him what he calls "modest epistemological confidence" as a historian. On one hand, Noll notes that his "increased confidence in the truthfulness of historic Christianity . . . has almost completely freed my mind from skepticism about the human ability to understand something about the past."[5] On the other hand, it also serves as "a powerful check to blithe overconfidence in the capacities of historical knowledge."[6] Christian doctrine helps him make sense of this important balance between two sides, "for if the heart of Christianity is the incarnation of God the Son, so the heart of historical knowledge is its duality between universal certainties and culturally specific particularities."[7] It certainly does not involve the separation of one's spiritual emotions from one's historical mind.

STANLEY HAUERWAS—A CHRISTIAN THEOLOGIAN AND ETHICIST

Stanley Hauerwas provides a model of someone influenced by a community of academic models. As previously mentioned, Hauerwas is a widely

---

3. Mark A. Noll, *The Scandal of the Evangelical Mind* (Grand Rapids: Eerdmans, 1994) ix.

4. Ibid., 252.

5. Mark A. Noll, "Teaching History as a Christian," in *Religion, Scholarship and Higher Education: Perspectives, Models and Future Prospects: Essays from The Lilly Seminar on Religion and Higher Education*, ed. Andrea Sterk (Notre Dame, IN: University of Notre Dame Press, 2002) 163.

6. Ibid.

7. Ibid., 164.

recognized theologian and ethicist who serves on the faculty at Duke University Divinity School. Born and raised a United Methodist (now an Episcopalian) in Pleasant Grove, Texas, Hauerwas routinely writes about his experiences growing up in Texas as the son of a bricklayer. His writing thus often includes an eclectic mix of bravado, working-class values, and an attention to detail yielded by someone committed to a particular craft. Hauerwas attended Southwestern University in Georgetown, Texas as an undergraduate and did his graduate work at Yale University. Hauerwas then moved to Augustana College (IL) and the University of Notre Dame before coming to Duke.

The time he spent at Notre Dame played a critical role in shaping his Christian life. In fact, despite studying theological ethics, he would offer that "At Notre Dame, I began the slow, agonizing, and happy process that has made me a Christian."[8] In particular, he would suggest he became an Anabaptist Catholic. Anabaptists, embodied in groups such as the Amish, Brethren, and Mennonites, emphasize the life and teachings of Christ and the practice of the Christian faith as essential in determining theological commitments. Catholics, in this particular sense, emphasize the legacy of theologians (such as the medieval theologian Thomas Aquinas) and the cultivation of the virtues through particular practices. Several of Hauerwas' colleagues at Notre Dame introduced him to the wisdom of Catholic thought. However, while he was in South Bend he also met an Anabaptist theologian by the name of John Howard Yoder and eventually embraced much of Yoder's thought. While Hauerwas argues the seeds of his Christian identity were planted during his childhood in Texas, his time at Notre Dame propelled him to argue that "there is no substitute for learning to be a Christian by being in the presence of significant lives made significant by being Christian."[9]

This slow, agonizing, yet happy process propelled Hauerwas to chart a course for theological ethics that has found widespread impact in the church and the Christian university. Hauerwas adamantly argues for the central role of the church in the lives of Christian people. Such a role would not only supersede other commitments in life such as to the nation-state, but also the way modern human beings see themselves first as individuals and second as members of some other group such as the body of Christ. Hauerwas thus

8. Stanley Hauerwas, *Hannah's Child: A Theologian's Memoir* (Grand Rapids: Eerdmans, 2010) 95.

9. Ibid.

relentlessly seeks to re-center people's primary identity as Christian people and then reorient the manner in which they live out their lives.

In *A Community of Character: Toward a Constructive Christian Social Ethics*, a book that is arguably one of his most influential, Hauerwas explains "that the only reason for being Christian (which may well have results that in society's terms seem less than 'good') is because Christian convictions are true; and the only reason for participation in the church is that it is a community that pledges to form its life by that truth."[10] Theology for Hauerwas is thus not just a set of abstract principles but a message that lays claim on how we understand ourselves and the ways we live out our lives.

In particular, Hauerwas argues one of the most critical convictions concerning how Christians are to live out their lives is a commitment to nonviolence. In *The Peaceable Kingdom*, Hauerwas contends, "Any proposal about the Christian life is not just a group of ideas about how we might live, but a claim about how we should live if we are to be faithful to the God of Israel and Jesus."[11] Nonviolence is thus not just an abstract principle to which Christians commit themselves but dismiss at points when the practical details of life prove overwhelming. In contrast, Hauerwas believes the joy yielded by nonviolence is "the simple willingness to live with the assurance of God's redemption."[12] While Hauerwas had unpacked the logic of this argument in relation to past crises, the attacks launched by members of Al-Qaeda on September 11, 2001, proved to be an immediate test. In the end, Hauerwas argues that the lens through which Christians should view their response to the violence of that day is not simply through the violence of that day, but rather by the nonviolent response issued by Christ about 2,000 years ago in terms of the crucifixion.

JEAN BETHKE ELSHTAIN—A CHRISTIAN POLITICAL SCIENTIST

A picture of courage and conviction, Jean Bethke Elshtain, who passed away just before this book was published, made considerable contributions to how both scholars and the general public view politics. Stanley Hauerwas thought so and once remarked that he always admired Jean Bethke

10. Stanley Hauerwas, *A Community of Character: Toward a Constructive Christian Social Ethic* (Notre Dame, IN: University of Notre Dame Press, 1981) 1.

11. Stanley Hauerwas, *The Peaceable Kingdom* (Notre Dame, IN: The University of Notre Dame Press, 1993) 149.

12. Ibid., 147.

Elshtain's "energy, her intellectual vitality, and her courage. It is not easy being a feminist against abortion, but Jean is a person of strong conviction who is not about to compromise in the interest of gaining the approval of those who style themselves as morally enlightened."[13] That praise proves all the more significant given the friendship Hauerwas once shared with Elshtain had come to an end over their irreconcilable views of the actions taken by the United States following the events of September 11, 2001.

On many levels, there is no denying Elshtain was a remarkable person. Growing up in northern Colorado, Elshtain was stricken with polio as a child and bore the marks of her battle with that illness. After graduating from Colorado State University, Elshtain headed east to complete her graduate work at Brandeis University. She served on the faculties at the University of Massachusetts and Vanderbilt University before moving to the University of Chicago.

In an unpublished speech entitled "The Ups and Downs of a Christian Political Philosopher," Elshtain remarked that "In my work in those early years, I did not identify myself as having any particular religious beliefs, in part because I did not know if I had them."[14] When looking back, she discovered that her work was replete with references and appeals to the works of theologians. She would find her work became read perhaps even more by theologians than political philosophers. For example, her first book and arguably still her most significant, *Public Man, Private Woman: Women in Social and Political Thought*, includes such references in large numbers. As her career progressed, figures such as Augustine, Thomas Aquinas, and John Calvin would prove to be frequent conversation partners for Elshtain in a number of works.

Her fusing of theological perspectives into political theory can be observed in Elshtain's *Sovereignty: God, State, and Self.* In this work, one initially given as the Gifford Lectures (the equivalent of the Nobel Prize for theologians and philosophers) she explores how perceptions of sovereignty have been transferred over the course of modernity from God, to the state, and eventually to the individual person. Elshtain concludes by making the argument that "the notion of the modern self leads to the destruction of the human person . . . . Nihilism confounds creator and created in the same

---

13. Stanley Hauerwas, *Hannah's Child*, 271.

14. Jean Bethke Elshtain, "The Ups and Downs of a Christian Political Philosopher" (unpublished manuscript) 8.

blind fury."[15] In essence, by freeing ourselves from both God and the state, we enslave ourselves to the navigation of a sea of endless choices. Augustine would thus argue our hearts are now doomed to be restless for something they will never find on their own.

Perhaps Elshtain's most controversial book (and the one harboring some of the ideas that dissolved the friendship she once shared with Hauerwas) came in response to the choices made following the events of September 11, 2001. In *Just War Against Terror: The Burden of American Power in a Violent World*, Elshtain argues, "Unless America proposes to close itself up behind its borders (something impossible in any case given the porousness of those borders) and revert to isolationism, we can and we must become the leading guarantor of a structure of stability and order in a violent world."[16] Underneath this argument is an appeal to what some have labeled as the just war tradition and to arguments made by theologians such as Augustine. Although this view made her unpopular with a good portion of her academic brethren, Elshtain's energy, intellectual vitality, and courage sustained her in the midst of those attacks. Whether one agrees with her or not, Hauerwas' assertion concerning how little use Elshtain has for views that are fashionable provides an example of Christian courage in the academy.

JOHN POLKINGHORNE—A CHRISTIAN SCIENTIST AND THEOLOGIAN

For the young Christian scientist looking for a model of how someone might combine his or her identity as a Christian and a scientist in fruitful ways, one obvious place to start is with the example of John Polkinghorne. What makes Polkinghorne unique is his dual training as both a scientist and a theologian. He first attended the University of Cambridge where he studied mathematics as an undergraduate and was shaped significantly by his involvement in the Christian Union, a nondenominational campus group. Called to be a scientist, he studied mathematical physics as a doctoral student at Cambridge under the famous Nobel Prize winning physicist Paul Dirac. Later, after a fellowship at the California Institute of Technology

15. Jean Bethke Elshtain, *Sovereignty: God, State, and Self* (New York: Basic Books, 2008) 227–28.

16. Jean Bethke Elshtain, *Just War Against Terror: The Burden of American Power in a Violent World* (New York: Basic Books, 2003) 173.

and a lectureship at the University of Edinburgh, he returned to teach at Cambridge until he was forty-nine.

At that time, he experienced a second calling. After twenty-five years as a physicist, he left his prestigious position at Cambridge to train for the Anglican ministry as a priest. He made the change not out of disillusionment with the field of physics but with the view that "I simply felt that I had done my little bit for particle theory and the time had come to do something else."[17] After receiving his education in theology, his dual training gave him a unique perspective to contribute to the dialogue about the relationship between Christianity and science; thus, while even in his early parish ministry he started publishing his first works about the relationship between Christianity and science. Three years later, he returned to Cambridge as Dean and Chaplain of Trinity Hall and later President of Queen's College.

From that academic position, he continued publishing numerous books about the whole range of concerns regarding the relationship of science to religion, theology, and Christianity. The titles of some of Polkinghorne's works published since that time give some idea of the variety of topics he addresses: *Science and Religion in Quest of Truth*; *Testing Scripture: A Scientist Explores the Bible*; *Theology in the Context of Science*; *Exploring Reality*; *One World: The Interaction of Science and Theology*; *The Intertwining of Science and Religion*; *Science and the Trinity: The Christian Encounter with Reality*; *The God of Hope and the End of the World*; *Faith, Science and Understanding*; and *Belief in God in an Age of Science*.

The theme of many of these works is Polkinghorne's quest for truth, and the role that he believes science and Christianity play in this quest. On one hand, he observes that "science describes only one dimension of the many-layered reality within which we live, restricting itself to the impersonal and general, and bracketing out the personal and unique."[18] Since he shares a concern with the unity of knowledge and truth, he recognizes that "even within its own domain science cannot yet tell a fully integrated story." Thus, he believes other disciplines, particularly theology, are needed to gain a larger picture of reality.[19] On the other hand, while Polkinghorne writes to

---

17. John Polkinghorne, *From Physicist to Priest: An Autobiography* (London: SPCK, 2007) 71.

18. John C. Polkinghorne, *Exploring Reality: The Intertwining of Science and Religion* (New Haven, CT: Yale University Press, 2005) ix.

19. Ibid., x.

encourage scientists to take theology seriously and not dismiss it without a hearing, he also writes "to encourage religious people to take science seriously and not to fear the truth that it brings."[20]

For Polkinghorne, the two fields must recognize their contributions and limits. For instance, while Polkinghorne believes theology should still be considered the queen of the sciences, "[Its] regal status lies in its commitment to seek the deepest possible level of understanding. In the course of that endeavor, it needs to take into account all other forms of knowledge, while in no way attempting to assert hegemony over them. A theological view of the world is a total view of the world. Every form of human understanding must make a contribution to it."[21] From Polkinghorne's perspective, theology must draw upon and depend upon science as it develops this comprehensive worldview.

Thanks to the professors he encountered, in many ways Jacob is on a comparable path that the individuals discussed in this chapter also followed. He became dissatisfied by various conditions that tried to keep him loving God with all his heart, soul, mind, and strength, and, in turn, loving his neighbor. These professors placed, as Mark Noll put it, the cross of Christ at the center. Jacob's calling led him into the field of business. His professors, like those highlighted in this chapter, graciously helped him to see the various ways the Christian faith called into question both the theories and the practices that defined the fields he was studying. In order to do so, all of Jacob's identity, just like the figures considered in this chapter, played an active and integrated role. His vocational education shaped not merely his identity but also every other facet of his being. As a result, Jacob saw the needs of the villagers in Africa he encountered differently. In time, he also came to see the economic needs of his own community differently. The promise of the Christian university resides in its ability to make just such a difference in all of its students.

QUESTIONS FOR DISCUSSION

1. In what ways, if any, do you think your institution facilitates relationships shared by various dimensions of your identity? For example, in what ways does chapel relate your heart to your mind? The classroom?

20. John Polkinghorne, *From Physicist to Priest*, 134.

21. John Polkinghorne, *Polkinghorne Reader: Science, Faith and the Search for Meaning*, ed. Thomas Jay Oord (Philadelphia: Templeton, 2010) 94.

The out-of-class experiences? In what ways, if any, do you think your institution hinders those relationships?

2. In what ways, if any, has your church facilitated relationships shared by various dimensions of your identity? In what ways, if any, do you think your church hinders those relationships?

3. How do you perceive of the secular versus the sacred? Are there certain spaces on your campus that are specifically designated (even if that designation is unstated) as secular? Sacred?

4. In what way(s) if any, is the gospel political?

5. Do you believe that evangelical culture has undergone some form of intellectual scandal? If so, in what ways?

6. Do you believe that even within the Christian university, truth is often accommodated to what might be deemed fashionable? If so, what forms? In what ways are such pressures exerted?

Chapter Seven

Learning to Live

A community that argues ideas only in the classroom, a teacher whose work seems a chore, a student who never reads a thing beyond what is assigned, a campus that empties itself of life and thought all weekend, an attitude that devaluates disciplined study in comparison with rival claimants on time and energy, a dominant concern for job preparation— these can never produce a climate for learning.[1]

—ARTHUR F. HOLMES, *THE IDEA OF A CHRISTIAN COLLEGE*

SERGIO'S GIFTS AS A student and as a leader were evident from a young age. He was always at or near the top of his class in terms of his academic performance. At the same time, he was almost always willing to wear the mantle of responsibility that came with representing his peers in student government. In junior high, several of his friends decided Sergio should run for student body president. He declined but they persisted and eventually won him over with an appeal to his developing sense of duty to them and their fellow classmates. Now with a track record in politics, his friends did not have as difficult of a time persuading him to run for class president as a freshman, sophomore, and junior in high school. By the time he was a senior, no one really seemed interested in running against him for student body president. On one level, he possessed an uncanny

1. Arthur Holmes, *The Idea of a Christian College* (Grand Rapids: Eerdmans, 1987) 101.

ability to understand and communicate what was important about earning an education. On another level, who would be willing to challenge the well-established campaign staff that was firmly behind Sergio and dated back to the days they were all freshmen?

Now in college, Sergio's leadership gifts quickly became evident to a new group of peers. Sergio ran for class president again but then was persuaded at the end of his sophomore year that he should consider running for student body president and thus possibly serve two terms. Their Christian university had come to be one Sergio and his peers greatly appreciated. However, its recent burst of growth had left the university with several challenges that seemed to escape many one-term presidents. In particular, their university was facing somewhat of an identity crisis. While it still thought of itself as a small college where everyone knew one another, 4,000 undergraduates and half again as many graduate students made that perception unrealistic. As a result, Sergio ran and won on a platform of bringing people—students, faculty, staff, and administrators—together for conversations about what made their university unique and what the people who called it home all had in common.

One of the first initiatives that Sergio and members of his cabinet decided to pursue was what they referred to as "One Book, One Community." Like many other campuses, Sergio thought their university should become a venue where common conversations were able to take place. As a result, he thought one way to begin those kinds of conversations was to ask every member of the community to read the same book and then gather together in a variety of venues to discuss it. The reading would take place over the summer (even incoming students would get a copy of the book at registration) and then everyone would have the opportunity to participate in a variety of discussion venues (some voluntary and some required). The highlight of the time they would spend together would be when the author of the book would come to campus and deliver an address in the chapel services.

Being a knowledgeable politician, Sergio knew he needed to form a committee that could refine this idea and then communicate it to the campus community. His cabinet began by proposing names of people to invite to serve on this committee. Two students from each class were chosen. Thinking alumni might want to participate in some manner, the vice president for alumni relations was selected. The remaining slots were filled by the provost, the vice president for student development, the director of residence life, and the chair of the English department. Once ratified by his cabinet, Sergio went to work in an effort to persuade these individuals they nominated to serve. Given the purpose of the program and the fact that a nearby information technology firm had even offered to underwrite the costs, almost everyone was supportive.

The first holdout, however, came in the form of the chair of the English department. Dr. Richard Bartholomew was a medieval literature scholar of some renown, had managed to double the number of majors and faculty members in his department over the course of the last ten years, and was in the process of developing a proposal for a PhD program. Sergio had enjoyed Dr. Bartholomew's world literature class and was certain he would be eager to serve on a committee where the purpose was to draw the campus community together around a common read. Unfortunately, Sergio was quite surprised by the response he received. Dr. Bartholomew's initial question was "What kind of book would they read?" After Sergio offered that they were thinking about a novel, Dr. Bartholomew went into a rather lengthy discussion concerning the perils of allowing such reading to be given over to non-experts. As the chair of the English department, he then shared with Sergio that while he admired the underlying convictions driving such a program, he could not support it. In the end, Dr. Bartholomew argued, "Studying these texts is hard work and needs to take place in the proper environment."

Disappointed by the response he received, Sergio was optimistic that his next appointment, with the director of residence life, would be different. Keith Alban had served as the head of the residence life area for almost fifteen years. As a result of the recent student enrollment growth, he had led the construction of three new residence halls and the complete renovation of two others. He was also supportive of the underlying convictions behind what Sergio was proposing. However, he too had some reservations. As the university had grown, Mr. Alban argued, "The residence halls have become places where students can escape the pressures of the work they faced in the classroom." While he wanted to maintain spaces where students could study if they chose to do so, Mr. Alban was not sure he wanted the residence halls to host reading groups as part of their programming.

Dismayed by these two responses, Sergio was not sure where to go next. How was he going to be able to launch this program if the chair of the English department and the director of residence life were opposed to it? Something inside Sergio said that these commitments held by Dr. Bartholomew and Mr. Alban were problematic. However, he was not sure how to explain the core problem and whether to persist with an idea he and the rest of his cabinet were optimistic would find overwhelming support.

DISTINCTIONS DEFINED

Unfortunately, Sergio's experience is not an uncommon one in today's university. As institutions have grown, so has the need to divide responsibilities amongst more specialized sets of experts. In Sergio's case, he found these expectations. English faculty members teach English. Residence Life administrators work with students in the residence halls. At best, the size of their institutions keeps the separate entities from coordinating their efforts. At worst, their perception of their own expertise keeps the leaders of these entities from seeing any value in partnering with other members of the university community. For whatever reason, students are left to navigate an institution which appears to house independent nation-states requiring them to learn a new language each time they cross a border. While universities employ phrases such as "seamless learning," students are left to wonder what, if anything, their experience in one class has to do with their experience in another. Or, on an even larger scale, what their experience in class has to do with their experience out of class.

When such divisions form, students are left to perceive of their experiences in class and performing class-related activities, however fragmented, as the practices involved with being a learner and their experiences out of class as disconnected from learning. Such a perception comes with a variety of challenges that undercut the integrity of any university and arguably even more so for a university that bears the name Christian. An example of one challenge can be found in Tom Wolfe's novel, *I Am Charlotte Simmons*, where he tells the story of an underprivileged yet academically accomplished student who leaves the confines of her small town to attend DuPont University, a fictitious yet presumably elite institution of higher learning. Upon her arrival, Charlotte is overwhelmed by the manner in which the students live their lives. While they take their studies seriously, her colleagues view these efforts as necessary sacrifices that will one day allow for lives of professional and thus financial privilege. Once they are done learning, the students commit themselves in earnest to meaningless play, often succumbing to directionless forms of excess such as alcohol-induced sex.

In a desperate attempt to fit in at DuPont, Charlotte succumbed to the seemingly inevitable ritual of drinking in excess. When offered vodka with a splash of orange juice, Charlotte wondered: "Maybe if she could just finish it, she really would feel better. After all, alcohol was supposed to relax you. In any case, maybe tonight she wouldn't feel so much like she was on the outside looking in."[2] Finish it she did, along with an array of other drinks offered to her by her male hosts. The end result of the evening's experience resides somewhere in the murky tragedy that initially began as something referred to as "hooking up." To the depraved observer, the end result was that Charlotte lost her virginity that night in what has become an all-too-common collegiate ritual. To the astute observer, the end result was that Charlotte lost her virginity as the victim of sexual assault—arguably the most egregious outgrowth of a culture consumed by the practice of the work hard/play hard mentality.

While Tom Wolfe's story is one of fiction, I desperately wish this story was one divorced from reality. However, according to One in Four, a non-profit organization dedicated to combatting sexual assault, "One in four college women report surviving rape or attempted rape since their fourteenth birthday."[3] Contrary to perceptions that sexual assaults are most commonly perpetuated by strangers, the same organization reports that "57% of rapes happen on dates." Echoing Tom Wolfe's tragic literary account even further, One in Four contends that "75% of the men and 55% of the women involved in acquaintance rapes were drinking or taking drugs just before the attack."[4] Wolfe reportedly became interested in writing *I Am Charlotte Simmons* after hearing stories from his daughter, Alexandra, about such occurrences on her own college campus, Duke University. In the case of this novel, the line between art and reality is tragically difficult to differentiate.

If asked to assess the work hard/play hard mentality that defines too many university campuses (and dare I say Christian university campuses as well) today, Augustine would likely not be surprised by the tragic consequences. Given the nature of his own conversion to Christianity, Augustine would quickly argue that all of life must fall under a common commitment. As a result, at the beginning of book 9 of *The Confessions*, or shortly after Augustine recounts the details of the moment he gave himself over to

2. Tom Wolfe, *I Am Charlotte Simmons* (New York: Farrar, Straus, and Giroux, 2004) 445.

3. One In Four, "Sexual Assault Statistics," http://www.oneinfourusa.org/statistics. php (accessed May 29, 2012).

4. Ibid.

Christ, he writes, "Let me praise you in my heart, let me praise you with my tongue. *Let this be the cry of my whole being. Lord, there is none like you.*"[5]

In order to fulfill its calling to cultivate a love of God and neighbor, our whole being must be the focus of the university and the programs it offers. Common worship prioritizes and cultivates these loves, and the experiences that take place in the classroom provide them with considerable theoretical and practical depth. However, the learning experiences that take place outside of the classroom, in spaces such as the residence hall, the student center, and the intramural field, become valuable arenas for the practice of lived theology. As a result, the Christian university comes closest to fulfilling its mission when the curricular and the cocurricular, following the lead set by common worship, work in an integrated fashion to cultivate the whole being of all community members.

BRIEF HISTORY OF STUDENT DEVELOPMENT/LIFE/AFFAIRS

Depending upon your campus, one of the largest divisions of educators is housed in an area often referred to as student development, student life, or student affairs. Small philosophical distinctions are attached to one reference versus the other. However, for my purposes, all three essentially refer to the same entity and are more aptly referred to as the cocurricular. For most of the history of higher education in America, the efforts now led by cocurricular educators (such as orientation, career services, residence life, student activities, student discipline, student health services, student leadership programs, etc.) were conducted in some manner by faculty members. Prior to the late 1800s/early 1900s, faculty members often lived on campus and supervised all aspects of the student experience. As the university grew and as what we now refer to as the research university emerged, faculty members were pressed into more specialized areas of service related to their academic disciplines. Their professional standing thus came to be vested in efforts they made to establish themselves as experts in a particular field. At the same time, the growing size of their institutions made it difficult for any one person to shape and guide the student experience.

As a result, a new class of student deans, advisors, and other support staff for students began to surface on college campuses and eventually formed a vocational identity in the 1930s. Often initially referred to

5. Augustine, *The Confessions*, trans. R. S. Pine-Coffin (New York: Penguin, 1961) 181.

as student personnel administrators, these individuals began to take hold of the responsibility for all aspects of the student experience beyond the classroom. Given the mounting pressures upon them to publish and/or present the results of their work, some faculty were eager to yield duties that lay beyond the purview of their classrooms, laboratories, and studios to this new class of colleagues. Responding to confusion surrounding what then constituted student personnel work, in 1936, W. H. Cowley, then a professor of psychology at The Ohio State University, would argue that "Personnel work constitutes all activities undertaken or sponsored by an educational institution, aside from curricular instruction, in which the student's personal development is the primary consideration."[6] As institutions continued to grow larger, the formal nature of these professionals, the services they provided, and the structures they created would only expand.

Following waves of unprecedented growth in higher education that took place in the 1960s, 1970s, and 1980s, some cocurricular educators became concerned about how the focus of the services they were providing were philosophically and structurally divorced from the larger educational purposes of the institutions. To rectify this problem, twelve senior members of what is known as the American College Personnel Association (ACPA) gathered in the fall of 1993 to draft a document that came to be referred as the "Student Learning Imperative." Presented by George Kuh, then a higher education professor at Indiana University, to the membership of ACPA in the spring of 1994, this document opened with the assertion that "The student affairs division mission complements the institution's mission, with the enhancement of student learning and personal development being the primary goal of student affairs programs and services."[7] While still a long way from achieving these goals on many campuses, the emergence of the phrase "cocurricular" can arguably be traced back to this document.

Student personnel administrators now often see themselves as partners with the faculty in the education of students. Such efforts have begun to decrease the excesses fostered by distinctions made between learning and play, but there is arguably a long way to go. In what follows, I will argue that even more is at stake for the Christian university committed to eradicating that distinction.

6. W. H. Cowley, "The Nature of Student Personnel Work," in *Student Affairs: A Profession's Heritage*, ed. Audrey L. Rentz (Lanham, MD: American College Personnel Association, 1994) 59.

7. American College Personnel Association, "Student Learning Imperative: Implications for Student Affairs," http://www.acpa.nche.edu/sli/sli.htm (accessed May 29, 2012).

THE PERILS OF THE LEARNING/PLAY DISTINCTION

As already argued, a separation between the curricular and the cocurricular leaves students with the impression that arenas such as the classroom, laboratory, or studio are places of work and such areas are supervised by the faculty. In addition, it leaves students with the impression that arenas such as the student center, the residence hall, and the intramural field are places of play, are loosely supervised by student life professionals, and are not arenas for learning. On the Christian university campus, it also breeds two other distinctions that undercut the very mission of the institution.

First, a distinction between academic learning and play also allows students to view their academic lives as governed by a certain set of vocational rules, virtues, and practices to which they must commit. It then allows them to view their play as private and governed by a different set of rules disconnected from any larger vision of human flourishing. In general, those rules ask little to nothing of people in terms of who they are to become (for example, a loving neighbor, a faithful friend, a gracious host, a charitable human being, etc.). In contrast, they simply ask students to not act in ways that interfere with the play or well-being of other members of the community. Lurking just beneath the surface of this expectation is the belief that one's Christian identity and its associated story, virtues, and practices are a private matter and somehow not relevant or permissible in public.

In *Bad Religion: How We Became a Nation of Heretics*, Ross Douthat, a columnist for *The New York Times*, goes so far as to label this approach a heresy that poses a greater challenge to Christianity than atheism. In particular, Douthat contends Americans are often consumed with the "Cult of the God Within." With figures such as one-time television star Oprah Winfrey serving as one of its high priestesses, this cult depersonalizes God in order to make God accessible (and arguably more comfortable—for example, who needs the God of the Old Testament represented in the form of the prophets and demanding repentance?). Christ is then reduced to just a great teacher who offers guidance for us as we make our way on our own individual path. In the end, Douthat argues, "the apostles of the God Within focus on internal harmony—mental, psychological, spiritual—as the chief evidence of things unseen."[8] God's existence is not confirmed through other forms of revelation God gives us found in nature, scripture, and tradition. In contrast, it only comes from somewhere inside each one of us.

8. Ross Douthat, *Bad Religion: How We Became A Nation of Heretics* (New York: Free Press, 2012) 217.

The tragic result of this approach to learning is the separation of Christianity from both the curricular and the cocurricular. For example, in a psychology class, reason based on a secular story and setting becomes the dominant means of knowing truth and the only one suitable in such a public forum. Professors propose material in such a manner and students are trained to evaluate the material accordingly. If religious faith is discussed, it is simply viewed as the personal reflections of a singular individual and thus not transferable to others. In the residence hall, faith may be valued and even encouraged. However, the means for evaluating its significance are determined by each individual on his or her own. The residence hall becomes a place where students can chose to live in ways they think are best for them as long as those ways do not interfere with the well-being of other students. Students' lives are then neatly prescribed but ultimately something less than Christian.

THE COCURRICULAR: A REALM FOR LIVED THEOLOGY

The previous sections have needed to explore more of what the cocurricular is not—an environment focused on play, the private dimensions of life, and a narrow view of Christianity. I would now propose that what makes the cocurricular arena unique in comparison to the curricular and common worship is the way it allows for educators to design and deliver exercises for lived theology. When designed well, the argument can be made that students can learn just as much, if not more, about their calling to love God and their neighbors in spaces such as the residence hall, the student center, and the intramural field as they can in the classroom, the laboratory, and the studio.

One advantage cocurricular educators at the Christian university have is that they can draw upon lessons afforded in any number of classes on campus and extend them even further into the realm of lived experience than most faculty. Part of this advantage stems from the nature of the experiences afforded to cocurricular educators. For example, a director of leadership programs can consider any number of social and psychological theories, as well as the overarching theology, in her interaction with students serving in student government roles. As a result of the role theology plays, the Christian university is an inherently interdisciplinary community. However, most faculty members are only asked to consider the contributions afforded by a handful of disciplines at most. In this particular scenario, answers to real-life questions (as in most of life) often transcend disciplinary boundaries. As a result, the director of leadership programs often has no choice but to draw upon wisdom from a host of disciplines, with theology serving as the queen of the sciences, as she advises her students.

Another advantage cocurricular educators have is that the programs they facilitate inherently have a lived dimension to them. While the theology one learns in common worship services and in classes may have similar dimensions woven into them, by their very nature cocurricular programs do not (or should not) allow any distinction to separate theory from practice. In essence, theories can and should be considered at length. However, at the end of the day, life demands that we make decisions. Faculty members have practices such as service-learning at their disposal. However, someone serving as a director of leadership programs knows the group she is advising must make decisions that often impact the entire student body. As a result, the success of any student government program is dependent upon not only the depth of thought but also the firmness of the decisions the group is able to make in the light of the university's mission and on behalf of their peers.

Finally, one other advantage cocurricular educators have over curricular educators is the nature of the spaces they supervise and the amount of time they spend with the students. Faculty members often meet with students in prescribed spaces and at prescribed times. While that grants faculty members a certain sense of structure their interactions with students often need, it also runs the risk of leaving students with the impression that those lessons only apply in those spaces and at those times. In contrast, cocurricular educators have the opportunity (or the challenge, in the case of an emergency phone call at 3:30 a.m.) to speak into students' lives on an almost constant basis.

Returning to my example, a director of student leadership programs often works with the same group of students for a whole year and, in the case of some students, for the entirety of their student careers. In addition, she might meet with those students in any number of venues and at any number of times. The advice she is able to offer comes over longer periods of time and in any number of contexts. In the end, those forms of interaction are more closely approximated to the way people live their lives as whole beings. While cocurricular educators may have other advantages at their disposal, their roles are not superior to the roles played by faculty members. In contrast, both groups need to work together in order to provide students with the kind of education a Christian university is charged with cultivating.

Fortunately for the university community Sergio was elected to serve, he and his fellow cabinet members persisted and launched their "One Book, One Community" initiative. In the provost and the vice president for student affairs, Sergio found discussion partners who were eager to break up any sense of separation between spaces reserved for learning and play. Together, they all realized that the success of their university to cultivate a love of God and neighbor went beyond the particular commitments represented by the departments they led. They sought to launch a program that would engage the whole community and what Augustine referred to as "the whole being." In the end, Dr. Bartholomew would prove influential in helping the group select its first book and developing the reading guide. In addition, Mr. Alban would prove to be critical in structuring the discussion groups and identifying the spaces where those groups could meet. Without one another (along with the rest of the members of the committee), Sergio's vision would not have come to fruition and his university would have proven to be a little less than it was called to be.

QUESTIONS FOR DISCUSSION

1. What programs, if any, on your campus serve as a means to draw people with diverse sets of commitments and responsibilities together? Why are they drawn to those programs?

2. What barriers, if any, separate programs in the curricular and cocurricular realms from one another?

3. In what ways, if any, are distinctions made between work and play on your campus? What then can be done to rectify those distinctions?

4. Are any spaces and/or programs on (or off) your campus deemed public or private in nature?

5. How are reason and faith perceived on your campus? Are there any spaces and/or programs that are perceived as being solely defined by one in absence of the other?

6. What programs on your campus draw upon more forms of student identity than most? What partnerships, if any, do those programs share with other offices and/or programs on campus?

7. In what way(s) can your campus more fully engage the community and, at the same time, engage the whole being of the people that call it home?

Chapter Eight

The End of Academic Freedom

Freedom of thought is the freedom to think for oneself with the faith one has and the beliefs and the values to which one is committed. In this sense neither faith nor intellect can be forced but must be free.[1]

—ARTHUR F. HOLMES, *THE IDEA OF A CHRISTIAN COLLEGE*

IN MAY 2012, JUDITH Lynne Hanna, a Senior Research Scholar in the Departments of Dance and Anthropology at the University of Maryland, published *Naked Truth: Strip Clubs, Democracy, and a Christian Right.* In this book, Hanna reportedly:

> [T]akes readers onstage, backstage, and into the community and courts to reveal the conflicts, charges, and realities that are playing out at the intersection of erotic fantasy, religion, politics, and law. She explains why exotic dance is a legitimate form of artistic communication and debunks the many myths and untruths that the Christian Right uses to fight strip clubs.[2]

On one level, her work argues for the legitimacy of forms of dance that take place in establishments often referred to as strip clubs. She lobbies against popular perceptions that the majority of individuals who perform in these

1. Arthur Holmes, *The Idea of a Christian College* (Grand Rapids: Eerdmans, 1987) 62.

2. Judith Lynne Hanna, personal webpage, http://judithhanna.com/books/naked-truth/ (accessed May 14, 2012).

clubs are under the influence of some form of narcotics. In addition, she contends any number of routes lead performers to get onstage, ranging from a dare to the allure of extra income. Finally, she contends these clubs are not all dens of crime but rather that "exotic dance is an industry that has become increasingly upscale with a broad clientele."[3]

On another level, Hanna seeks to expose what she believes are aggressive and often unethical tactics used to suppress the forms of performance that take place in these clubs. In particular, she singles out what she refers to as CR-Activists or politically engaged individuals identified with what she refers to as the Christian Right. According to Hanna, the underlying reason why these individuals engage in this form of activism is to impose their vision of morality upon others. In essence, these efforts are representative of a wave of responses to the gains in individual liberties secured during the 1960s and early 1970s. Obsessed now with regaining some semblance of "Dominionism," Hanna believes these CR-Activists are "Obsessed with dominion over the nation, [with] movement adherents believ[ing] that expansion of state control over sexuality is key to creating a salutary environment for their children and making way for the ideal state."[4] Is Hanna's scholarship justifying strip clubs an expression of what is often referred to as academic freedom even if she worked at a Christian university?

In a very different environment from the one where Judith Lynne Hanna practices her work as an anthropologist, Steven Johnson, the president of a Christian university in the Southeast, found himself facing a dilemma. The current issue of the student newspaper included a front page, above-the-fold story about outrage to the message shared by a recent chapel speaker. This guest speaker had made some remarks the previous week about how the role of women was to be limited to the home (or other private spaces, as Jean Bethke Elshtain explains) and that life beyond the home was the purview of men. Compounding this message was the speaker's assertion that any challenge to this view was biblically deemed sinful. Students responded to it adversely, as did a number of faculty members.

The dilemma President Johnson was facing was that a board meeting was scheduled to take place on campus that week and members of the board often liked to read the newspaper as one way of obtaining an appreciation for what was occurring on the campus and what was important to the students.

3. Judith Lynne Hanna, *Naked Truth: Strip Clubs, Democracy, and a Christian Right* (Austin: University of Texas Press, 2012) 186.

4. Ibid, 10.

Knowing some of his board members appointed by the sponsoring denomination may agree with the views shared by the speaker, President Johnson was concerned by how discussions might go at the meeting. While President Johnson shared in these reservations, he worried about whether these board members would have concerns over the fact that students who expressed these kinds of views were currently enrolled at the university. In addition, would these board members become anxious about the fact that the university employed faculty members who also expressed these kinds of views? To date, relations with members of the board he served had proven to be quite peaceful. However, similar issues had gotten away from presidents on other campuses and led to decisive forms of action being taken by board members that involved policies impacting students and personnel decisions impacting faculty members.

As a result, President Johnson chose to ask his executive assistant to collect all available copies of the issue of that newspaper and recycle them prior to the arrival of members of the board. While doing so, a couple of students (who were surprisingly up early) spotted her collecting the papers. Rumors quickly spread about President Johnson's intentions and, rumors being what they are, some were accurate while some were inaccurate. The board meeting would pass without controversy but students and faculty members persisted in raising their concerns. Had President Johnson failed to honor the spirit of academic freedom that governed his campus as a Christian university?

A PROBLEM OF DEFINITION

The problem with answering these questions is a matter of definition and, as I argue, hinges on one's choice of prepositions. Academic freedom is critical to the practice of any institution of higher learning and is essential for the Christian university to fully realize how it is called to cultivate a love for God and neighbor. Love cannot be forced. However, competing differences in how academic freedom is understood make it difficult for us to sort through the competing answers. Looking back to the previous century, the introduction to a book entitled *Regulating the Intellectuals: Perspectives on Academic Freedom in the 1980s* indicates "there is little consensus regarding the meaning of academic freedom although there is agreement that it is something worth protecting."[5] Unfortunately, little has changed since that time. How is it that something as important as academic freedom is so ill-defined?

At the heart of this problem is the fact that despite its cherished place in our contemporary vocabulary, a word such as "freedom," like most words, changes in terms of its meaning over time. Part of the reason for those changes in this particular case is that perceptions of what it means to be human have also changed considerably since the establishment of the university in the Middle Ages. The ahistorical manner in which we approach these issues means we often fail to grasp those changes unless we pause long enough to consider them.

As a result, it is not surprising an anthropologist such as Hanna seemingly operates with the assumption that the human "object" she studies and the networks of meaning in which that "object" is embedded are stagnant. In addition, President Johnson, however conflicted he may have been over that particular issue, chose to operate with assumptions concerning the political immediacy related to that particular situation versus the longer view of the history of his own institution, the Christian university, and the importance of robust academic debate.

The most common definition of academic freedom is the one provided by the American Association of University Professors (AAUP). In a statement dating back to 1940 and still in place today, the AAUP offers:

> College and university teachers are citizens, members of a learned profession, and officers of an educational institution. When they speak or write as citizens, they should be free from institutional censorship or discipline, but their special position in the community imposes special obligations. As scholars and educational officers, they should remember that the public may judge their profession and their institution by their utterances. Hence they should at all times be accurate, should exercise appropriate restraint, should show respect for the opinions of others, and should make every effort to indicate that they are not speaking for the institution.[6]

While this statement offers a considerable amount to digest, its primary focus is on the need for freedom for members of the academic profession in order for them to do their work. In essence, in order to pursue truth

5. Craig Kaplan, *Regulating the Intellectuals: Perspectives on Academic Freedom in the 1980s* (Westport, CT: Praeger, 1983) 6.

6. American Association of University Professors, "1940 Statement of Principles on Academic Freedom and Tenure," http://www.aaup.org/AAUP/pubsres/policydocs/contents/1940statement.htm (accessed May 14, 2012).

within one's field, one must be free to follow wherever that inquiry may lead. In exchange for this form of freedom, scholars are encouraged to exercise various forms of responsibility in relation to their pursuits. As a result, a university should not repress the work of scholars nor should scholars wander too far afield from their own area(s) of expertise.

Returning to my earlier reference to prepositions, I want to focus on the significance of the word "from" in the third line of this excerpt from the statement from the AAUP. In our current social and political context, we often think of freedom in terms of freedom from some external agent that may seek to suppress our range of choices. Given the depraved nature of the human condition, securing freedom for people in the face of powers that may otherwise oppress them is critical to human flourishing. However, such an understanding should not become so fixed in our mind as to be the only way freedom has been and should be understood. The dilemma here is that while it protects the rights of individuals, it fails to orient us toward the end or *telos* of academic freedom. As a result, the AAUP statement as written is not insufficient but is simply incomplete. Such a statement should not only tell us what we are free from but also free for—in essence, it needs to also answer the question, "What is the end of academic freedom?"

TAKING THE LONG VIEW OF FREEDOM'S HISTORY

In order to cultivate an appreciation for the end of academic freedom, we must first look back and see the sources of freedom and how those sources relied upon a specific vision of what it means to be fully human. The work of Orlando Patterson, a faculty member in sociology at Harvard University, proves to be helpful at this point.

In *Freedom in the Making of Western Culture*, Patterson writes, "The long history of freedom . . . is merely a long series of footnotes to the great civilizational text that was already complete, and almost fully edited, by the end of the Middle Ages."[7] The roots of freedom, he claims, reside with the Greeks, how the Romans incorporated the Greek legacy, and the way Christianity adapted to Roman culture and spread into the Middle Ages. Like many scholars who looked at this question, Patterson factors in the critical role slavery played in relation to perceptions of freedom. However, he also argues women played a considerable role in terms of shaping and

7. Olando Patterson, *Freedom in the Making of Western Culture* (New York: Basic Books, 1991) xvi.

reshaping how freedom was to be understood. In the end, he argues that "As long as Christianity survived, so, at least in spiritual form, would the deep Western commitment to the ideal of freedom."[8]

Moving to the end (and unfortunately skipping over an impressive array of historical detail) Patterson argues freedom is not only the greatest cultural contribution of Western culture but also made possible some of the greatest horrors. As a result, each generation that inherits this cultural legacy must come to terms with its value as well as the threats allowed by freedom that might be unleashed. He concludes by arguing that this very irony that freedom makes possible was most radically realized in the crucifixion—what he refers to as "the ultimate veneration of choice."[9] In order to fully appreciate that legacy, any notion of freedom must not only realize what the cross makes us free from but also what it makes us free to become.

FREEDOM IN THE CHRISTIAN EDUCATIONAL TRADITION

Augustine's *Confessions*, mentioned in earlier chapters, provides an early example of a Christian educator's answer to the question, "What freedom is for?" Written retrospectively, roughly the first half of Augustine's work details the various delusions he found himself chasing—vice, fame, influence, and the shortsighted solace pedaled by false teachers. Each delusion would grant momentary peace but leave Augustine with an even greater appetite for the next offering. At the close of this journey, Augustine recounts how he turned to the apostle Paul's Epistle to the Romans (13:13–14) and read "Let us behave decently, as in the daytime, not in orgies and drunkenness, not in sexual immorality and debauchery, not in dissension and jealousy. Rather, clothe yourselves with the Lord Jesus Christ, and do not think about how to gratify the desires of the sinful nature." At this point, Augustine not only came to know Christ but also became truly free, as his appetites were now focused upon loving God and his neighbor. God's grace through Christ allowed him to rightly order his loves and to give him freedom from the disordered loves he previously knew and lived.

Augustine's outlook would go on to shape one of the earliest architects of what would come to be known as the university, Hugh of St. Victor (1096–1141). Hugh was a student and then eventually a teacher at the Augustinian Abbey of St. Victor founded by William of Champeaux just

8. Ibid.

9. Ibid., 406.

outside of Paris. In his *Explanation of the Rule of St. Augustine*, Hugh opens by acknowledging, "Dear Brothers, before all else, love God and then your neighbor, because these are the chief commandments given us."[10] In order to attend to those commandments, Hugh believes we must be free from the false apparitions of freedom which once enslaved us. In order to properly love God and neighbor, we must be truly free in the manner only established by the cross of Christ.

In the *Didascalion*, Hugh contends the very nature of education is a formative process, a process which aids human beings in their efforts to reconnect with the divine likeness afforded to them as a result of being created in God's image. While this image was corrupted by the fall, the work of Christ makes possible once again our reconnection and increasing conformity to it. He then goes on to argue, "The more we are conformed to the divine nature, the more do we possess Wisdom, for then there begins to shine forth again in us what has forever existed in the divine Idea or Pattern, coming and going in us but standing changeless in God."[11] Wisdom only comes when we are truly free in Christ to once again allow the "divine Idea or Pattern" to shine forth through us. It cannot come when we are enslaved to our own passions and the erratic array of directions they might drag us.

As a result, the medieval university was an institution committed to restoring this likeness through any number of activities. Amongst these activities, the ones that often get the most attention are the various components of the curriculum. For example, as previously indicated, part of what Hugh of St. Victor asks students to submit themselves to is found in areas historically known as the *trivium* and the *quadrivium*. For Hugh, the "trivium [grammar, dialectic, and rhetoric] is concerned with words, which are external things, and the quadrivium [arithmetic, geometry, astronomy, and music] with concepts, which are internally conceived."[12] While Hugh would acknowledge students would go on and study a mechanical art or the creation of an "artificer's product," the heart of the curriculum and the role of all of the liberal arts was to reorient students in relation to God's original divine pattern. The focus of Hugh's vision for the university, a legacy which would persist for hundreds of years, was to help students recapture the di-

---

10. Hugh of St. Victor, *Explanation of the Rule of St. Augustine*, trans. Dom Aloysius Smith (n.p.: Revelation-Insight, 2008) 24.

11. Ibid.

12. Hugh of St. Victor, *The Didascalion of Hugh of St. Victor: A Medieval Guide to the Arts*, trans. Jerome Taylor (New York: Columbia University Press, 1991) 75.

vine freedom lost in the fall but once again made possible by the cross of Christ—freedom to once again truly love God and neighbor.

THE RISE OF THE "RESEARCH" UNIVERSITY

Over time, the focus on freedom within the university shifted from a concern with freedom "for" to freedom "from." One scholar who helped foster this shift was Immanuel Kant. Kant was a German philosopher who sought to establish a system of thought that would place human reason at the center of the educational experience.

Risking considerable oversimplification (as Kant is notoriously complex), woven into Kant's understanding of what it means to be human is the perception that reason is a capacity, with certain limitations and possibilities, that can be acquired by all. In other words, Kant does not believe one's particular setting or story alters, deforms, or transforms reason. For instance, he does not view the depravity of the fall or the redemption of the cross as being central to how one's reason is shaped. In fact, in Kant's new story concerning reason, reason is understood to have a salvific role that will save us from our core problem of ignorance (versus our disordered will and loves).

In order for human rationality to operate optimally, it must not find itself hindered in any manner—most especially by external agencies or organizations. The unfettered practice of reason is now what allows human beings to fulfill their promise. As one Kant scholar noted,

> According to Kant, for reason to save us it needs freedom. For example, Kant writes: It is absolutely essential that the learned community at the university also contain a faculty that is independent of the government's command with regard to its teachings; one that, having no commands to give, is free to evaluate everything, and concerns itself with the interests of the sciences: one in which reason is authorized to speak out publicly.[13]

As a result, one of the most critical qualities of a university is its ability to afford community members the freedom to follow their inquiry wherever that inquiry might lead. At times, that inquiry might yield questions and/or answers that prove reassuring to members of other communities (such as

13. Immanuel Kant, *The Conflict of the Faculties*, trans. Mary J. Gregor (Lincoln: University of Nebraska Press, 1992) 27–28.

the government in this particular case). At other times, that inquiry might yield questions and/or answers that prove to be disconcerting. Regardless, the ability to follow that line of inquiry and to do so in an environment free from intrusion became a definitive quality of the modern university.

Shortly after Kant penned these words, the German research university inspired by Kant's vision would become the model for all other higher education institutions in the West. The breadth and depth of thought it unleashed would yield some of the greatest scholars of the day and thus attract students from around the world—including students from the United States seeking what were coming to be known as graduate degrees. These students would then return to places such as the United States with not only the formal lessons afforded to them by their disciplines but also the definitive qualities of the educational culture they experienced.

Their influence contributed to the formation of the AAUP's first statement on academic freedom in 1915 (followed up by the previously cited statement from 1940). The result, as Columbia University professor Walter P. Metzger argued, was that "Academic freedom was the end: due process, tenure, and professional competence were regarded as necessary means."[14] Organizational structures and processes were put into place that would not only grant academic freedom to scholars deserving it but also protect them from the kinds of pressures that could hinder their efforts and thus the search for truth.

ACADEMIC FREEDOM—A TALE BORN OF TWO TREES

Part of the challenge with defining the role academic freedom is to play in the life of the Christian university is that while Immanuel Kant disregarded many of the critical components of the university set in place by Hugh of St. Victor, Hugh of St. Victor did not imagine at the time a university as large and complex as today's Christian university. In no way is this assertion intended to indicate that the present form of the university is better than its predecessor. In contrast, the two forms are just different. The creation of knowledge that is now an essential part of university life was not formally part of what Hugh had in mind. However, the lessons he offered still play an important role in determining the nature of academic freedom.

---

14. Richard Hofstadter and Walter P. Metzger, *The Development of Academic Freedom in the United States* (New York: Columbia University Press, 1955) 481.

In Genesis 2:15–17 we read, "God took the man and put him in the Garden of Eden to work it and take care of it. And the Lord God commanded the man, 'You are free to eat from any tree in the garden; but you must not eat from the tree of the knowledge of good and evil, for when you eat from it you will certainly die.'" While this passage points toward the spiritual death that Adam and Eve and all of their descendants would endure, it also points to the need for a second tree upon which the possibility of freedom would be offered once again to all individuals created in God's image. In Luke 23:26–43, we read of the events that took place on that second tree—the crucifixion of Christ and the choice placed before two thieves. While these two thieves represent historical figures, they arguably represent the opportunities before all of us. One thief chose to embrace his own depraved form of freedom and reject Christ. The other thief chose to embrace Christ and thus embrace the true freedom Christ offers to all.

Hugh of St. Victor rightfully understood that in order to be truly free to love God and love one's neighbor, one must first make the choice presented to these two thieves. By making the same choice made by the second thief, it is now possible for us to appreciate our true calling. Only once that form of freedom is in place can one fully appreciate what is at stake in terms of the work of Immanuel Kant. Apart from any understanding of what the utilization of freedom is oriented toward, shortsighted fits of anarchy are the end results. Kant's argument that the scholar is to be free from external agencies that might otherwise hinder exploration is critical. However, that scholar must first have a keen appreciation of the *telos* his or her scholarly pursuits are designed to serve.

In all fairness to Judith Lynne Hanna, she serves at the University of Maryland and her work is best judged by whatever criteria are in place at that institution. However, for the sake of argument, I am going to contend that both she and President Johnson failed to fully appreciate what is at stake when it comes to academic freedom. In Hanna's case, her work represents one form of academic anarchy. To read through her work is to be confronted with the reality that an academic climate that lacks an understanding of what freedom is to be ordered toward will generate this form of work. While Hanna might brand me as a CR-Activist, what concerns me the most about her work is that she never recognizes that establishments such as strip clubs are venues where human beings are reduced to, or choose to reduce themselves to, mere objects. As a result, such a form of reduction undercuts any reasonable aspiration of human flourishing regardless of how she might choose to spin her arguments.

President Johnson's efforts should also raise questions. His campus is in need of a venue to have a constructive conversation about the words shared from the pulpit in its chapel. Students and advisors who work with the newspaper are charged with reporting information deemed newsworthy to that campus community in accordance with the canons of journalism. If those canons were violated in some manner, that issue would need to be addressed with the students and the advisors. However, just because the news presented in that issue might prove to be unsettling for members of the board does not mean that copies of the newspaper bearing those concerns should disappear. In the end, President Johnson's decision represents the opposite of academic anarchy: academic totalitarianism. He might be able to avoid having this conversation with members of his board. However, he has also now sent the message to members of his community that certain issues are not to be raised regardless of the reason for raising them.

The details defining academic freedom are ultimately embedded in the details harbored by prepositions. The Christian university is an environment where the pursuit of truth demands scholars be free from external agencies. At the same time, the Christian university is also an environment where the pursuit of truth demands its scholars know to what end they are free. Failure to recognize one of those two prepositions leaves the Christian university unproductive by virtue of standards for now in place for institutions bearing the name of "university." Failure to recognize the other leaves the Christian university susceptible to various forms of academic anarchy or totalitarianism that plague so many campuses today.

QUESTIONS FOR DISCUSSION:

1. How do you define academic freedom? In what way(s), if any, does that definition compare with the one presented in this chapter?

2. How does your campus community define academic freedom? In what way(s), if any, does that definition compare with the one presented in this chapter?

3. In what way(s) does your definition of academic freedom compare with how your campus community defines academic freedom?

4. In what way(s) does the Christian university of today represent challenges Hugh of St. Victor might never have organizationally envisioned?

5. Please think of a research project you are currently conducting or on which you are about to embark. In what way(s) do both forms of freedom need to be in place in order for your project to meet its intended goals?

Chapter Nine

When Diversity Is Not Enough

Christian love is a moral virtue, not just, and sometimes not at all, a warm quality to one's feelings. It is the sort of moral concern for others' well-being that motivates hard and sacrificial work. What love does on the inward side of human relations justice attempts on the outward side by securing people's rights and opportunities as equitably as possible.[1]

—ARTHUR F. HOLMES, *THE IDEA OF A CHRISTIAN COLLEGE*

FROM THE DAY SHE was born, her parents knew Cassidy was extraordinary. While her laugh warmed their hearts, her smile melted them. As she grew older, she always seemed to have a joyful spirit that won over almost any individual she met. Caregivers in the church nursery would occasionally concede Cassidy was their favorite. Waitstaff members in restaurants could not help but dig out an extra set of crayons, bring an additional breadstick, and even offer a scoop of ice cream on the side to the child who would engage them with a never-ending array of insightful questions. Cassidy's parents even became accustomed to the possibility that it might take them two to three times longer than the average parents to work their way through the grocery store as senior adults would often stop them in the middle of the aisle so they could talk to the child who captured their attention in a matter of seconds. Of course, Cassidy was always willing to engage

1. Arthur Holmes, *The Idea of a Christian College* (Grand Rapids: Eerdmans, 1987) 96.

in any conversation, at any time, and with anyone her parents would allow. As she grew older, her parents could tell she had a unique gift of listening and thus knowing how to respond in a way that indicated she had known even a perfect stranger for years.

As she grew older, Cassidy's circle of admirers only grew wider. Her magnetic personality won people over, but her unwillingness to complain about the fact that she was visually impaired from the day she was born amazed them. Everyone should recognize life is a gift and God's grace is what sustains us. For Cassidy, such a perspective defined how she came to live her life every minute of every day. Not being able to see people meant she learned to listen and depend upon the gift of hearing in ways others could often not cultivate over the course of a lifetime of efforts. She valued people and the ways God was represented in their lives. Given she could not see people, she learned to do what we should all do first—listen. In just a few spoken words, Cassidy knew if someone was excited, sad, or anxious even if the words themselves did not detail those emotions. However odd it may seem, visual impairment thus proved in some ways to be a gift to Cassidy as she was able to see into people's hearts in ways often betrayed by the eyes of the sighted.

As one could guess, being visually impaired in a sighted world also came with some significant challenges. While teachers in preschool and elementary school were quite welcoming to Cassidy, they had never worked with a visually impaired child. Cassidy and her parents were patient, but teachers had to learn not only to alter how their classrooms were ordered but also how they taught. Physical spaces and pedagogical practices that reflected the diversity of needs and abilities of the children in the room became paramount. When a teacher would point to an item on the board, he or she could no longer simply say, "What do you think of this?" and assume the children would all be able to immediately identify the item to which they were referring. Books with braille options were added to the library. Art projects and displays became more tactile in nature. The process was slow but one that proved to be rewarding for all of the teachers and students where Cassidy went to school. As a result, Cassidy was "mainstreamed" in terms of her education from day one. She never assumed her disability would keep her from pursuing an education in ways comparable to the rest of her classmates.

Music always proved to be an interest to Cassidy, and Mrs. Reed, the choral music director at her high school, took a special interest in helping

Cassidy cultivate her voice. Cassidy had many emerging gifts but her ability to inspire people with her sung voice was becoming more evident. Mrs. Reed had never worked with a visually impaired student before but that did not dampen her zeal. Cassidy could not read standard forms of printed music but Mrs. Reed not only learned to acquire sheet music in a form of braille, she also learned to read it herself. As a result of these efforts and the encouragement Mrs. Reed offered her, Cassidy quickly became recognized in her region for her voice. The crowning achievement in her high school career came when Cassidy was able to play one of the leads in her high school's annual musical. While unable to dance in ways comparable to some of her other classmates, Cassidy filled the role of an operatic narrator and received a standing ovation from the audience on both nights the musical was presented. When asked by a local reporter about whether the response Cassidy received from the audience was due to the fact that she was visually impaired, Mrs. Reed quickly responded, "No. We simply gave Cassidy the same opportunity to succeed as any other student. She has a gift and she worked hard to cultivate that gift to the best of her ability. There is no reason to believe a visually impaired student cannot sing as well as a sighted student."

Unfortunately, college would initially prove to be a different story for Cassidy. While the disability services director at the Christian university where she enrolled proved to be very helpful, a couple of faculty members were initially unwilling to grant her the accommodations she rightfully deserved. One philosophy professor claimed that allowing Cassidy to take the exam in the testing center in the disability services office "gave her an unfair advantage." An economics professor argued that granting such accommodations simply allowed students such as Cassidy to "languish in their laziness." Part of his job as an economics professor was to thus "teach her to work hard just like any other student." Although Cassidy's voice professor had proven to be just as supportive as Mrs. Reed, these other kinds of experiences compelled Cassidy to think about dropping out of college.

Hearing of her frustration, the dean of the chapel, Dr. Watkins, talked with her personally and persuaded her to stay. He acknowledged the university had a ways to go in order to fully appreciate all of its students. However, he also encouraged her to realize she had some truly unique talents that needed to be shared with the university community in order for it to realize its full potential. If she withdrew, he said their campus "would be less than what God had uniquely designed it to be."

Unbeknownst to Cassidy, Dr. Watkins gave a homily at the Advent service for faculty that year entitled, "Learning to Welcome the Long-Expected Christ." As an African American, Dr. Watkins indicated that the university community had made great strides to make members of various ethnic groups welcome on the campus. They had also made great strides to welcome women to the once all-male campus and people from all economic classes. However, he argued, "What have we done to welcome the long-expected Christ who walks amongst us in the guise of persons with disabilities?" The end of his argument was that "We are able to catch glimpses of the diverse array of God's identity in the various ways it is not only represented in people created in God's image but also present in the very nature of Christ's body. How do we then welcome the long-expected Christ?"

A little more than three and a half years later, Cassidy was a senior and had thrived in ways she could not have imagined that first semester. Faculty members learned to appreciate her, and other visually impaired students were now enrolled and following in her footsteps. Her magnetic personality won over the hearts and minds of her classmates and especially the young man to whom she was now engaged. She had served as the academic vice president for the student government association under a wildly popular president, Lisa, who had also become her roommate and best friend.

Unfortunately, tragedy would strike at the end of spring break that senior year. Lisa, while driving back to campus, was hit by a drunk driver who had drifted over the center divider and struck her car in a head-on collision. Although transported by helicopter to a local hospital, physicians and nurses on staff were unable to save her. News of the tragedy spread across the campus. Student life administrators, faculty members, and Dr. Watkins were quick to meet with students and help them process their grief.

Upon hearing the news, however, Dr. Watkins' first visit that Saturday night was to Cassidy. They cried together, prayed together, and then went out to talk with other young women living in that residence hall about Lisa's death. At a meeting the next night with Dr. Watkins, members of the student government association decided they would hold a memorial service in Lisa's honor on Monday evening—the first day the community would be together again as a whole following spring break. In a standing-room-only event in the campus chapel, tributes were given by the university president, Lisa's parents, some of her closest friends, the former student government association vice president and now acting president for the remainder of the school year, and Dr. Watkins. The service then closed with the efforts of a talented vocal-performance student singing Horatio Spafford's timeless hymn, "It is Well with My Soul." Mustered by a young woman who had faced so much adversity and had now lost her best friend, not a dry eye was to be found in the chapel by the time she concluded her solo performance. A wound opened by the loss of a beloved friend would never heal this side of eternity. However, the unique gift of Cassidy's voice brought hope to faces she would never see but whose hearts she knew well.

THE FALL OF DIVERSITY

American higher education as well as the church is littered with stories of struggle in order to create a wider circle of appreciation for the diverse gifts present amongst members of the created order. Race, class, and gender have sat at the center of these discussions for almost 200 years, or, perhaps a better estimate might indicate 2,000 years. In *The Christian Imagination: Theology and the Origins of Race*, Willie James Jennings, a professor at Duke University Divinity School, argues that because peoples during the modern era "had jettisoned Israel from its calculus of the formation of Christian life, [they] created a conceptual vacuum that was filled by the European."[2] As a result, a system of valuing people was generated by standards facilitated by the culture of the day versus the horizons established by the possibility of a people defined by a larger story of creation, fall, and ultimately Christ's redemptive sacrifice. Determinations were thus made concerning the value of people based upon race, gender, and class. Countless Africans were enslaved. Women were denied certain rights granted to their male counterparts. Members of lower social classes were pitied at best or ostracized at worst. In this newfound way of determining the value of human beings, persons with disabilities were often viewed as aberrations of the ideal versus expressions of the diverse ways God is present in the world.

While this chapter will explore these ideas and the ways they tragically linger into the present generation, it also explores why calls for diversity are often not sufficient. Visions for diversity often operate with an assumption of a spirit of individualism that too often manifests itself in one of two options. In its worst form, this perception of diversity breaks down into a practice often labeled as tolerance. In essence, we pledge not to hinder one another based upon reasons such as race, class, gender, and/or disability

2. Willie James Jennings, *The Christian Imagination: Theology and the Origins of Race* (New Haven, CT: Yale University Press, 2010) 33.

and we go on our merry way feeling morally sufficient. The problem that comes is that if we can fit ourselves with a pair of blinders, then we can master the ability of essentially ignoring one another. You do your thing. I do my thing. As long as we do not keep one another from doing our respective things, we are fine. Logistically, we may run into problems, as the planet we share only gets smaller. For much more important reasons, God may have higher expectations for us.

In its better form, appreciation for diversity may look like something I call "boutique tourism." For example, I dine in any number of ethnic restaurants with the comfort of individuals raised in those particular regions of the world. Or, I have read and understand what any number of feminist scholars are arguing and can even communicate the details of those arguments to my students. However, in the end, these expressions of the worlds in which others inhabit are simply worlds I pass through on my way back to the world I originally inhabited. Perhaps somehow my vision of the world should change as a result of these experiences. For much more important reasons, God may once again have higher expectations of us. In the end, visions of diversity often prove to not be enough because they lack the ability to bear witness to some larger *telos*.

THE REDEMPTION OF DIVERSITY AND THE CHURCH

For the Christian university, the end of diversity is neither tolerance nor some form of boutique tourism. In contrast, the end of diversity is an appreciation for the manner in which the image of God is present in all members of the created order and how that image is most fully present in the gathered presence of Christ's body, the church. In this view, an appreciation for diversity is expressed through the recognition that our well-being is not separate from the well-being of other members of the created order and Christ's body. We are only fully human when we realize just how much we need others and how much they need us. The church then grants a vision to the Christian university of what the body of Christ is to be and how its members are called to live.

As you likely already know, many college and university campuses that bear the name Christian were once inaccessible to a wide array of people. Persons who were white, male, of a certain class, and failed to possess any disabilities were viewed as potential students. Those institutions were called to serve them because the church also viewed those same students as future leaders. One could thus make the argument that the church was just as guilty of oppression as the colleges and universities. Or colleges and universities were perhaps even following the lead offered by the church.

For example, African Americans were once prohibited from sitting with whites in the church sanctuary during services in many congregations. In contrast, they were forced to sit in places such as a balcony or, in some cases, even prohibited from entering the sanctuary. On a personal note, when I was in college in the South, I became intrigued by the fact that so many historically African American congregations had funeral homes right next door. Eventually I asked a history professor why that was the case and he explained to me that the white funeral homes in town at one time refused to bury African Americans. As a result, several African American churches established funeral homes so their people could secure a proper burial.

Women were often given very specific roles that reflected the roles of the larger society. Churches were often defined along the lines of class structure and reinforced through various social customs. In his book entitled *The Bible, Disability, and the Church: A New Vision of the People of God*, Regent University professor Amos Yong writes about how the church, drawing from faulty readings of passages from Leviticus, once treated certain disabilities as curses initiated by God and as forms of judgment upon the individuals bearing the disabilities and/or upon their families.[3] As a result, the church has often acted counter to its calling to be an agent of liberation in a depraved world. Instead, it has chosen to mirror some of the worst qualities of that world and, in a number of cases, act as an agent of oppression.

However, acts of oppression the church has initiated have fortunately not proven to be too far away from the seeds of liberation the church is also capable of sowing. Charles Taylor, a philosopher who served the majority of his career on the faculty at McGill University, argues that "A number of strands in contemporary politics turn on the need, sometimes the demand, for recognition."[4] While recognition can lead to the liberation of certain peoples, "Nonrecognition or misrecognition can inflict harm, be a form of oppression, imprisoning someone in a false, distorted, and reduced role of being."[5]

3. Amos Yong, *The Bible, Disability, and the Church: A New Vision of the People of God* (Grand Rapids: Eerdmans, 2011) 24–29.

4. Charles Taylor, "A Politics of Recognition," in *Multiculturalism: Examining the Politics of Recognition*, ed. Amy Gutmann (Princeton, NJ: Princeton University Press, 1994) 25.

5. Ibid.

In the American context, one can argue the abolition of slavery and thus the initial liberation of African Americans was born out of the church. Groups such as Quakers and Wesleyans believed all people deserved the kind of recognition Taylor was describing because, in their opinion, each person was created in God's image. Charles Marsh, a theologian at the University of Virginia, argues in *The Beloved Community: How Faith Shapes Social Justice from the Civil Rights Movement to Today*, that "The pursuit of beloved community [as evidenced by the church] gave the civil rights movement its sustaining spiritual vision."[6]

In a comparable way, one could argue the women's rights movement in the American context was born out of the church. For example, in *Liberating Tradition: Women's Identity and Vocation in Christian Perspective*, Houghton College professor Kristina LaCelle-Peterson, notes that on July 21, 1848 a group of men and women met at the Wesleyan Methodist Chapel in Seneca Falls, New York to draft and eventually adopt what came to be known as the Declaration of Sentiments. "[L]argely fueled by their religious commitments," LaCelle-Peterson argues this document was not only framed upon the Declaration of Independence but also came to serve in a comparable way in relation to the establishment of the women's rights movement.[7] In an attempt to define a faithful way forward in our present day, Wheaton College professor Beth Felker Jones offers in *Marks of His Wounds* that perceptions of gender and past or present forms of oppression can only be "reordered through the body of Christ when we participate in the ecclesial life of that body."[8] As a result, not only was the women's rights movement launched in the church, its complete fulfillment may take place there too.

One could argue the church's track record in terms of class has gone better over the course of its history than its track record in terms of addressing race and gender. From the earliest of days, the Lord showed a pronounced concern for the poor and routinely enlisted the efforts of the prophets to defend the rights of the poor in the face of any number of kings who lost their way. For example, one can only imagine the look on Jeroboam's face when Amos pronounced, "This is what the Lord says: For three sins of Israel, even for four, I will not relent. They sell the

6. Charles Marsh, *The Beloved Community: How Faith Shapes Social Justice from the Civil Rights Movement to Today* (New York: Basic Books, 2005) 1.

7. Kristina LaCelle-Peterson, *Liberating Tradition: Women's Identity and Vocation in Christian Perspective* (Grand Rapids: Baker Academic, 2008) 188.

8. Beth Felker Jones, *Marks of His Wounds: Gender Politics and Bodily Resurrection* (New York: Oxford University Press, 2007) 108.

innocent for silver, and the needy for a pair of sandals. They trample on the heads of the poor as on the dust of the ground and deny justice to the oppressed" (Amos 2:6–7).

Christ's most famous of recorded speeches, the Sermon on the Mount, argues for not only the rightful recognition of the place of the poor in the kingdom of God but in the opinions of some theologians, Christ's priority for the poor. For example, in *Liberation Theology after the End of History: The Refusal to Cease Suffering*, Daniel M. Bell, a professor at Lutheran Theological Southern Seminary in Columbia, South Carolina, contends, "justice is fundamentally a matter of recreation and reconciliation, of living in communion and love."[9] While the church's track record on such matters is far from perfect, one can certainly argue no other entity has done more to provide services such as relief, health care, and education to members of society who would otherwise not have access to them.

Where the church's record is arguably the weakest, however, is in terms of its treatment of persons with disabilities. While Christ was committed to making "the lame to walk and the blind to see," the church has not always followed in his divine example. As previously mentioned, persons with disabilities were often thought to bear curses placed upon them as a result of their own efforts and/or efforts made by members of their family. While the church should never relent in its efforts to make "the lame to walk and the blind to see," at the same time the church should also bear witness to the fact that persons with disabilities are full bearers of the created image of God. Amos Yong thus argues the church needs to not only consider how accessible its programs (in terms of the venues being used and the manner in which the messages are being shared) are for people with disabilities, but also the sense of hospitality embodied by members of Christ's body. As a result, the goal for the church must be "the full inclusion of all and the reception of each contribution, resulting in the enrichment and edification of others."[10] In essence, persons with disabilities are not simply people to be cared for by the church, but full and complete members of its fellowship.

9. Daniel M. Bell, *Liberation Theology After the End of History: The Refusal to Cease Suffering* (New York: Routledge, 2001) 187.

10. Yong, *The Bible, Disability, and the Church*, 79.

DIVERSITY, THE CHURCH, AND THE CHRISTIAN UNIVERSITY

In what ways, then, do the church and the Christian university go about creating environments where the *telos* of diversity is appreciated? In terms of a student such as Cassidy, how does the person with a disability find him or herself as a full member of the university community? The answers are simple but unfortunately the solutions are complex. As previously argued, the defining experience of a Christian university is the practice of common worship. The Christian university seeks to continue to cultivate that sense of common identity in the members that join its community. Only then can students, faculty members, and administrators alike properly understand what it means to love God and love one's diverse neighbor made in the image of God.

How does this occur? Members of the university community come together to remember their true identity—as members of the church, they are parts of one body. Persons of different races, genders, socioeconomic backgrounds, and abilities join together in recognition of the fact that in this world they are not alone, but parts of something greater than themselves. We each bear burdens of depravity when we come in but we leave with hope anew in Christ's saving grace. Beth Felker Jones offers that "Only when the body is conceptualized firmly in reference to the body for which Christians hope, the body redeemed in Jesus Christ, can we account for the broken bodies of humanity."[11] By virtue of Christ's grace and the sacrifice paid for by his redeemed body, we are no longer held captive by our depravity. In contrast, we are able to see ourselves and one another as not only uniquely created by God, but also in God's image. Instead of striving to overlook or objectify critical dimensions of our identity such as race, gender, class, and disability, we are able to see them as diverse reflections of the image of God present in all members of the created order. To appreciate one another in this context is to then appreciate God's image.

One of the practical ways for a Christian university to model this reality would be to have a worship team that reflects the diversity we will find at the restoration of God's kingdom where we will find someone "from every nation, tribe, people and language, standing before the throne in front of the Lamb" (Rev 7:9). It should be no surprise that one finding from a study of

11. Jones, *Marks of His Wounds*, 10.

multiracial congregations found that that the racial diversity of the worship leadership team is correlated with the racial diversity of a congregation.[12]

While common worship on the Christian university campus may set the *telos* for diversity, curricular and cocurricular programs are also called upon to unpack in a variety of ways what such a form of appreciation might look like in both theory and practice. In a manner comparable to what Amos Yong proposed, professors should think about how accessible and how hospitable their classes might be to the students. For example, how accessible is my classroom, laboratory, or studio to students who represent diverse arrays of cultures, learning styles, backgrounds, and/or disabilities? By creating an accessible classroom, faculty members can then work on creating a hospitable classroom. Such a classroom is not simply vested in a space where students feel recognized, welcomed, and respected—although those three goals are all important. Such a classroom is also a space where a diverse array of opinions and perspectives are made to feel welcome even if part of the end result is to assess those ideas in the light of the larger goal of the university to orient members of its community toward the love of God and neighbor.

These same two aspirations also prove to be critical in relation to cocurricular programming efforts. Student life professionals serving in areas such as orientation, residence life, student programs, and career services should ask themselves, "How accessible are my programs and the spaces in which those programs are housed to students who represent a diverse array of cultures, learning styles, backgrounds, and/or disabilities?" Once those questions are answered, student life professionals can then ask, "How hospitable are my programs and the spaces in which those programs are housed?" At some level, appreciation for diversity meets at the intersection of programs and spaces that are accessible and hospitable. However, the full answer to those questions comes through the ways students also invest themselves as members of the Christian university community. When assessed, are they transformed in terms of how they view God, themselves, and their neighbors by these lived efforts? While our depraved nature will preclude the full transformation of our loves this side of eternity, the Christian university and the church which grants her an identity provide valuable glimpses of the life to come.

While few would argue that diversity is not a laudable goal for institutions of higher education, the real challenge emerges when individuals

---

12. Gerardo Marti, *Worship Across the Racial Divide: Religious Music and the Multiracial Congregation* (New York: Oxford University Press) 2012.

are charged with the task of identifying to what end such a goal is to be pursued. Some may point to tolerance while others may point to what I referred to as boutique tourism and one option may prove more desirable than the other. The Christian university, however, is called upon to appreciate those differences that may otherwise divide us if for no other reason than that they offer us glimpses of the God who created us all in God's very image. Such details are difficult to grasp because the complexity of the Christian university affords us with so many ways to bring them to life. In moments when we least expect them, the voice of a young woman can bring hope to the faces of members of a community she cannot literally see but knew in her heart. In those moments, when the love of God and neighbor become most evident, we can see the true *telos* of diversity for the Christian university.

QUESTIONS FOR DISCUSSION

1. What do you perceive is the *telos* of diversity? What do you perceive is the *telos* of diversity as communicated by your university community? If different from the telos of appreciation, in what way(s) is it different?

2. Diversity is often thought of in terms of race, gender, class, and disability. In what way(s) might those categories be sufficient sub-categories to think through in relation to diversity? In what ways might those categories be insufficient?

3. Assuming you are sighted, if you were to spend a day on your campus facing the same challenges persons with visual disabilities face, what might you encounter? What changes, if any, should be made to make your campus more accessible and hospitable to persons with visual disabilities? What role(s) could you play in bringing about those changes?

4. What role(s) does the practice of common worship play in terms of communicating the significance of diversity? In what way(s) does that message impact perceptions of diversity in the curricular venues such as the classroom, studio, or laboratory? In cocurricular venues such as residence halls or the student center?

Chapter Ten

The Global Christian University

*The primary purpose of a Christian college is not to insulate and
protect students, but to educate them as responsible Christians.*[1]

—Arthur F. Holmes, *The Idea of a Christian College*

They both sat there crying. All of us on the admissions committee
felt an uncomfortable sadness. The stories had sounded the same for
the past few days as we sat interviewing applicants to the Christian university in Russia where I was serving as a visiting professor. Many students had
high marks, wonderful recommendations, and great potential to be Christian leaders. However, few had the money or even the present possibility of
paying the $1000-a-year tuition, a fraction of what it would cost in North
America, without substantial help from the university.

This particular student sat crying with her single mother, who was ex-
plaining that because she makes $60 a month, she would not be able to pay
the $250 fee that this university required everyone to pay. I thought of my
students in the United States who might spend this amount on electronics,
gas, or weekend entertainment. My resigned, cynical self told me, "This is
how most of the world lives. Few get a chance to attend a university." My
heart, however, told me, "It's not supposed to be like this." And I couldn't
help but shed tears with them.

1. Arthur Holmes, *The Idea of a Christian College* (Grand Rapids: Eerdmans, 1987) 85.

My family had suffered that year in Russia. At that moment in Moscow, record heat drove the temperature inside our apartment into the mid-90s. While we kept the windows open, construction continued outside from 6:00 a.m. to 11:00 p.m. Our one-year-old never slept more than two or three hours at a time as a result of the noise, heat, allergies, and asthma we discovered he had. One time, we had to call friends at 3:30 a.m. to rush our son to the doctor due to an asthma attack. We missed air conditioning, America's rules concerning construction, and our car.

Yet, listening to this potential student, as well as a host of others share their financial struggles, I realized how little I knew about perseverance and suffering. One of my students told me bluntly that she found Americans complain a lot when they go through suffering. While teaching American history to Russian students, I was struck by the fact that this was not always the attitude of some early American Christians. One text I used contained this diary entry from Francis Asbury who rode over 300,000 miles on horseback during his life to share the gospel, "The water froze as it ran from my horse's nostrils this trip. I have suffered a little by lodging in open houses this cold weather, but this is a very small thing when compared to what the dear Redeemer suffered for the salvation of precious souls."[2] I had come to teach about this history. Yet I needed both Russia and the Russian students at this Christian university to remind me what it actually means to experience and live it. There is nothing like learning from the global Christian university.

WHY IS GLOBAL LEARNING IMPORTANT?

Among universities in North America, an appreciation for the need to form more globally connected students has grown. For example, in his book *Our Underachieving Colleges*, the previously mentioned former President of Harvard University, Derek Bok, claims one of the goals of university education is the preparation of students for a global society.[3] One finds this goal reflected in the mission statements of Christian colleges and universities

2. Mark Noll, *A History of Christianity in the United States and Canada* (Grand Rapids: Eerdmans, 1992) 173.

3. Derek Bok, *Our Underachieving Colleges: A Candid Look at What Students Learn and Why They Should Be Learning More* (Princeton, NJ: Princeton University Press, 2006) 225–54.

where over one third of the Council for Christian Colleges and Universities (CCCU) currently refer to some form of a globally oriented goal.

One of the obvious differences one can find, however, between secular and Christian higher education concerns the narrative and setting in which students are invited to think about global learning. Bok gives four specific reasons for this concern, all of which are related to students' identity as American citizens or future professionals: 1) the federal government or other business groups will require the service of foreign specialists; 2) Americans need to learn about our role in the world "to meet their obligations as citizens"; 3) college graduates may be international executives or professionals; and 4) understanding other countries helps students understand America and our political institutions and culture.[4] One could get the impression that global learning is really about helping the American government, American businesses, and American students.

Part of what makes the Christian university unique is the grandness of its vision. It envisions itself as an institution that helps students love God and love their global array of neighbors. Since Christian universities conceive of their task as developing this love in all humans who are made in the image of God, they serve humanity and not merely a particular politically defined government, business, or student body. Their guiding vision of what it means to be fully human is informed by their understanding of God and God's story of creation, fall, and redemption.

A GLOBAL AND INCARNATE GOD

God created the world and intended humanity to fill it. In fact, one might argue that in the biblical narrative, God blessed us with diverse languages to help us fill the earth.[5] As humanity continued to disobey, however, one finds God using a common pattern throughout Scripture. God chooses the particular to bless the local, and God wants his followers to share in that practice. For instance, God chooses Abraham and promises to make him a great nation, but he also promises "and all peoples on earth will be blessed through you" (Gen 12:3b). This global blessing involves two roles. First, Israel is to be a model to other nations by demonstrating what it means to be holy and just as God is holy and just. Second, Israel is also to love

4. Ibid., 226–27.

5. David I. Smith and Barbara Carvill, *The Gift of the Stranger: Faith, Hospitality, and Foreign Language Learning* (Grand Rapids: Eerdmans, 2000) 3–17.

those from other nations, the "strangers" in their midst, in the same way that God loves them. In fact, as God redeems Israel from Egypt, they are to remember their own story as a motivation for this love as God commands, "love him as one of your native born, love him as yourself, for you were aliens in Egypt. I am the Lord your God" (Lev 19:33b). This love involves showing them hospitality without giving up their identity. At different times, one finds Israel fulfilling these two roles. For instance, 1 Kings 4:34 states how "Men of all nations came to listen to Solomon's wisdom, sent by all the kings of the world, who had heard of his wisdom" as an example of Israel being a model and blessing to other nations.

Both of these themes are taken up in the New Testament. Here one finds the particular nature of global love exemplified most fully by God who loved the world and in Christ who demonstrated the particularity of love in concrete, physical ways and places. Or as John 1:14 states, "The Word became flesh and made his dwelling among us." Likewise, Jesus takes up the call of Israel to be a blessing when he tells his Jewish listeners in the Sermon on the Mount that they are "the light of the world" and "a city on a hill" which "cannot be hidden" (Matt 5:14).

As followers of Christ, Christians are called to demonstrate these same ideas as part of the body of Christ, the church, and in other Christian institutions. Consequently, the Christian church and the Christian University have had a long interest in globalization before the term became popular. When the early church started in Jerusalem, the Holy Spirit inspired its members to embark upon a more global vision. Just as God's commission to Adam and Eve was to fill the earth and subdue it, Christ told the early church, "you will be my witnesses in Jerusalem, and in all Judea, and Samaria, and to the ends of the earth" (Acts 1:8b). Since that time, the church has indeed spread to most parts of the earth. Today, God's Spirit still calls and inspires the church to be a global blessing.

THE GLOBAL VISION OF THE CHRISTIAN UNIVERSITY

Consequently, a Christian university does not take up the task of global learning simply to promote the interests of a particular nation-state or to help international businesses prosper (although those may be side effects). Instead, the Christian university seeks to be a blessing and a light to all the nations and peoples and to incarnate that blessing in a particular place and manner.

Historically, the Christian university started with this vision to some degree. Birthed with the help of the church in the Middle Ages (in fact, the only European institution older than universities is the church) universities spread throughout different countries in Europe, but they were initially understood as transnational institutions in service to the transnational church and the common good of humanity. They attracted and accepted students from all nations and were not bound or limited by national boundaries or identity. As one scholar notes, "During the first two centuries of universities the idea of a national university was quite unthinkable. A university then could not be associated with any particular nation."[6]

This transnational impulse meant that wherever the missionary work of the church expanded around the globe, universities and colleges soon followed. When a small group of Puritans began Harvard College in 1636, a mere six years after they arrived in what was to becomes Massachusetts, they were building on an institutional form with over 400 years of history. To give this some perspective, Harvard itself is still not even 400 years old today. Indeed, Harvard was not the first college or university in North America. That distinction belongs to the Pontifical University of Santa Domingo (1538) and the University of Mexico (1551) which were both established by the Catholic Church. The Catholic Church also helped establish the first university in South America, the University of San Marcos in Peru (1551). A little over forty years later, the first college of higher education was established in Asia by the Jesuits, the Colegio de San Ildefonso in the Philippines (1595). In fact, the Church helped establish the first colleges or universities on the majority of continents.

Certain revival movements within the church also played a key role in the growth of the earliest universities in specific countries. As previously mentioned, only three colleges existed in America prior to the First Great Awakening. In the time during and after the Awakening, half a dozen more would emerge. America's Second Great Awakening provided another important impetus for college growth as the number of colleges exploded from only 29 permanent Protestant colleges to 133 by 1861.[7] This growth included a variety of denominations that did not even have universities in Europe (Methodists—34, Baptists—25, and Congregationalists—21).[8]

6. W. J. Hoye, "The Religious Roots of Academic Freedom," *Theological Studies* 58 (1997) 417.

7. William C. Ringenberg, *The Christian College: A History of Protestant Higher Education in America*, 2nd ed. (Grand Rapids: Baker Academic, 2006) 59.

8. Ibid.

While both Awakenings unleashed a powerful educational impetus in America, they also proved instrumental in sparking the creation of the international missions movement both in America and in England. The Protestant missionaries supported by these groups soon created educational institutions around the world. In Africa, Protestant missionaries in several regions started the first African colleges, many of which still exist to this day. For example, Fourah Bay College (1826) founded by Christian missionaries would be, until 1948, "the first and only education institution in all of Anglophone Africa (outside of South Africa)."[9]

In Asia, missionaries from England and the United States played a key role in the creation of the earliest universities and colleges in India, China, Japan, and Korea. In India, missionaries helped establish one of the earliest Protestant colleges that still affirms its Christian identity (Scottish Church College, 1830). In China, English and American missionaries established thirteen Protestant colleges that formed some the first higher education institutions for both men and women.[10] In Korea, a Presbyterian group helped found Union Christian College in 1897, the forerunner of Soongsil University, the first national university. Overall, the Protestant missions movement sparked by the Second Great Awakening provided a tremendous impetus behind the creation of Protestant higher education around the world.

Unfortunately, many of these universities wandered away from the vision that helped give them birth in order to now serve lesser masters. Increasingly, many educational leaders during the nineteenth century thought universities should focus upon serving the nation. The result was that these institutions of higher education were seen as servants of a political state instead of a universal body of humanity. If globalization is considered something new, it is only because university education over the past two centuries was steeped in the cult of the nation-state. Today, as Bok illustrates, the idea still predominates that universities should serve the interests of a particular nation-state or the individuals and entities within it.

The Christian university is thus called to a different kind of love and learning. Loving God and others means reaching out to and learning about the world. Creative and redemptive learning requires figuring out

---

9. Y. G. M. Lulat, *A History of African Higher Education from Antiquity to the Present: A Critical Synthesis* (Westport, CT: Praeger, 2005) 209.

10. Jesse G. Lutz, *China and the Christian Colleges 1850–1950* (Ithaca, NY: Cornell University Press, 1971).

the challenging task of how to further our understanding of and incarnate love to diverse and particular human communities around the world. To do so, the Christian university must be involved in being a community that attracts and blesses the global stranger both within its home community and by sending students to incarnate Christ's love in the larger global community.

A LIGHT ON THE HILL

One of the best ways to be a light is to be an excellent university that creates and redeems learners and learning. Building a community can attract visitors that will be struck by the different approach to learning. For example, I was reminded of this fact when talking to a Russian professor at a secular Russian university where I also taught who had visited a group of Christian colleges and universities in the United States soon after the fall of the Soviet Union. He had been impressed with the Christian colleges and universities since their country did not have a similar institution at the time. He recounted how one of the things that struck him was that students had posters in their rooms with Bible verses and Christian sayings. Under communism, posters with Communist ideology were required to be hung in offices and classrooms. He marveled that these students actually placed these posters with Bible verses on their walls voluntarily. He had never experienced a community inspired by sincere belief that actually practiced and promulgated these beliefs without government force or compulsion.

Attracting and blessing the global visitor also has numerous educational benefits for those practicing hospitality. Developing the practice of Christian hospitality for international professors and students is one such benefit. While practicing such hospitality, students and professors learn about different ways of experiencing the world. I experienced the benefits of this hospitality while undertaking my doctoral work. During that time I interviewed a Russian graduate student attending a Christian institution who had grown up as a Christian in the Soviet Union. In the course of our conversation, I discovered the radical ways her early education experience was much different than my own. Her story also provides an example of how a different educational narrative and setting might lead one to treat a stranger.

> At age nine I moved to another school and nobody knew me, and nobody knew what kind of student I was. I was completely a

stranger to them. So they of course introduced me like, "She is a Christian so that is why she is not like [us], but we hope that she will be one." A teacher decided to try a new technique on me. [She] talked to [the] children, without warning me, to tell them not to talk to me. Kind of like they will boycott me, and then I will realize what it means to be on my own. So I came to school and said hello to everybody and nobody says back, "Hi." Everybody turned [his or her] backs on me laughs and so on. It was so horrible. [The] first day I kind of didn't realize yet. It was sort of like, it cannot be this. What they are doing? I came home and really cried much and told my grandma, "I don't want to go to school anymore." So I told her what was the matter. She was like, "We'll pray." I said, "That is good for you to say pray, but then I have to go and face this again." So the second day it was even worse . . . when you have class it is okay. But when you have a break and everybody runs and plays and talks to each other and no one talks to you at all. Like you are like a leper. I got really distressed. I came home crying. I thought: I am not going back. I just cannot be any possible hero. I am not Joseph and I am not ready to be Daniel yet. It was very hard for me. My grandma was very wise. She said, "You cannot be, but God can."[11]

Without inviting and welcoming a diverse array of students and faculty into our midst, we will miss the global perspective that we need in order to learn.

This kind of hospitality not only benefits learners, it can also expand the church's learning and memory. Scripture, particularly in the Old Testament, talks repeatedly about remembering what God has done by retelling and rehearing these stories. A Christian university in Ukraine actually made this part of the curriculum. It created an oral history project documenting the faithfulness of the underground church in Ukraine. It conceived of the project on one level as an instrument of faith development for students. Since the students were born after the time when the church was outlawed, they rarely heard about the faithfulness of Christian saints who persevered during the reign of communism. All of the theology students participate in a course about oral history in which they interview an older Christian who remained faithful during that time. The result has been that the students have conducted 2,000 interviews and collected 80,000 pages of transcriptions from people in the underground church. This type of creative and redemptive scholarship, performed by students, helps pass along the stories of the Christian models of faithfulness to the next generation. It is also an example of how we can learn from the practices of Christian universities around the globe.

11. Personal interview, December 5, 1995.

THE INCARNATIONAL APPROACH

In the process of becoming more "global citizens," students sometimes begin to disparage local connections, concerns, and allegiances. Yet, we do not become more fully human by denying our particular identities, including our national identity. In other words, an enhanced care and concern for the global community and the global church should not involve the same kind of love described by a doctor in Fyodor Dostoyevsky's *The Brothers Karamazov*:

> I love humanity . . . but I wonder at myself. The more I love humanity in general, the less I love man in particular. In my dreams . . . I have often come to making enthusiastic schemes for the service of humanity, and perhaps I might actually have faced crucifixion if it had been suddenly necessary; and yet I am incapable of living in the same room with anyone for two days together, as I know by experience. As soon as anyone is near me, his personality disturbs my self-complacency and restricts my freedom. In twenty-four hours I begin to hate the best of men: one because he's too long over his dinner; another because he has a cold and keeps on blowing his nose.[12]

Instead, God's love should, as Christ showed us, magnify our love for the particular—whether it is a particular person, family, neighbor, enemy, country, or even a particular aspect of nature.

As a result, Christian universities should create some of the best international studies and foreign language programs because they are designed to extend this particular love. Many Christian universities have already developed student study abroad programs that attempt this endeavor for these reasons.[13] One productive way to enhance these experiences is to partner with Christian universities around the world (which it appears only a few programs do). Such relationships can benefit both partners at various levels (students, faculty, and institutions). While global partnerships of Christian universities, such as International Association for the Promotion of Christian Higher Education (IAPCHE)[14] have begun, specific partnerships among

12. Fyodor Dostoyevsky, *The Brothers Karamazov*, trans. Constance Garnett (Grand Rapids: Christian Classics Ethereal Library, n.d.) 34 (http://www.ccel.org/ccel/dostoevsky/brothers.pdf).

13. For exemplary descriptions of these programs, see Ronald J. Morgan and Cynthia Toms Smedley, eds., *Transformations at the Edge of the World* (Abilene, TX: Abilene Christian University, 2010).

14. www.iapche.org.

various Christian universities are much more limited. Yet today outside of North America, over 580 universities exist in at least 73 different countries that affirm their Christian identity in their mission statement.[15]

It is in these countries where the Christian university is growing the most. For example, in the last decade, more Christian colleges and universities have started in Africa than in all other parts of the world combined. This continued creativity and growth at the global level now needs to be nurtured by partnerships with a worldwide church that once again cultivates institutions of higher education rooted in a global identity that stems from the universality of the church. Below are examples of just some of the benefits of this type of integrated global learning for students, professors, and institutions.

STUDENTS

Experiences with global Christian universities can change students' lives in ways that they might not experience in our own culture. I would not be where I am today without one of those experiences. When I was a student, I spent a summer in Thailand with a Christian parachurch organization interacting with students on college campuses about Christianity. During that time, I encountered an influential Christian professor in Thailand at one of the few Christian universities in the country. I noticed how this professor made a difference in the lives of her students in a country that had few Christians. Her example planted within me a vision of the difference a Christian professor can make in a secular context. God eventually used her example to call me to begin my teaching career as a professor at a secular university in a foreign country.[16]

While this type of learning experience from a global Christian university happened informally, creative ideas for more organized interaction would enhance these kinds of experiences further. At a Christian university in Ukraine, I found one illustration of how this type of partnership could occur. The university partnered with Christian ministries at North American

15. Perry L. Glanzer, Joel A. Carpenter, and Nick Lantinga, "Looking for God in the University: Examining Trends in Global Christian Higher Education," *Higher Education* 61/6 (2011) 721–55. For the most recent listings, see www.iapche.com.

16. Those interested in a similar calling may be interested in knowing that an organization exists that fosters such placements: the International Institute for Christian Studies (http://www.iics.com/).

universities to bring Canadian and American students to Ukraine for the summer. While both sets of students engaged in Christian formation and cultural exchange, the Ukrainian students were also learning English (and were required to speak English during the whole experience). The experience proved beneficial but difficult for both the North American and the Ukrainian students. Held at a remote setting, the Ukrainians, who could not afford to go to an English-speaking country for a month, were required to live their whole lives, including worship, meals, and recreation in an English-speaking context. For these students, it was challenging to be in a "foreign country."

For the English-speaking students, although they knew the language, everything else about the culture was new for them. The food, relational mores, teaching methods, different worship style, foreign leadership, and weather proved challenging and unsettling. Moreover, both groups learned from each other spiritually during times of worship, Bible study, and general communal life together. As one professor told me, "it's a way of bringing the university out into society." One could imagine a more formal partnership with a Christian university in which both sets of students received credit for classes about Ukrainian history and culture taught in English. In this case, the university proved incredibly creative in combining holistic forms of learning.

FACULTY

Faculty learning and teaching could also benefit immensely from these types of global partnerships. My own experience teaching at Christian and secular universities in Russia proved incredibly enriching. Teaching ethics in Russia proved to be quite different from teaching ethics in the United States. For example, I usually do not have to deal with the issue of bribery in the United States. In Russia, it was a major question. We learned to discuss creative ways of dealing with bribery (e.g., one student told about how her grandmother gave a Bible when a "gift" was expected instead of the usual bribe of vodka). I still keep a paper in my office by a student named Irene as an example of how Russian Christians had to deal with bribery:

> Some years ago my mother became pregnant when she was 43 years old. The doctors demanded a big bribe from my mother otherwise they refused to treat her. "You have to have an abortion," the doctor said. My mother faced this hideous obstacle . . . She made a decision to face the fire rather than compromise, but it was not easy, when all

the doctors were standing against her. When the moment of birth came no doctor wanted to help my mother, but finally a woman-doctor took the responsibility. My small brother was born. I hate bribery . . . Sometimes the circumstances of life are like a fire to us. So we need to learn how to face the fire rather than compromise. We have to choose to obey and to follow God, to have a relationship with God. We have to stand up for what we believe.

As a professor, this teaching experience stretched me to consider how to teach ethics in a whole new field of difficulty for local Christians in a unique way. It also opened my eyes to a whole range of models who exemplified what it means to love God in a context with challenges much different than my own.

The global context can also sharpen faculty and students as they face new questions about material that may seem quite familiar. In addition to ethics, I also taught courses in church-state studies. Reading Romans 13:1–7 (verses about the purpose of governing authorities and the Christians' response to them) with students from a different country proves quite stimulating. One former communist professor in Russia looked at me and asked after reading about submitting to authorities, "But what about Joseph Stalin?" Similarly, passages we discuss in an ethics class about caring for the poor suddenly are more noticeable or take on particular contemporary meanings when your students wear the same pieces of clothing to class for the entire week.

CREATING CHRISTIAN UNIVERSITIES

In many instances, the role that global partnerships among Christian universities can play has not been fully realized, particularly with regard to the creation of new Christian universities. A good example of this role concerns the story of the development of the first comprehensive Christian university on the continent of Australia. Oddly, while Christians started the first universities on most continents, the first universities in Australia were founded as non-theological institutions and the church did not play a central role. The formation of the University of Notre Dame Australia in 1989 marked the beginning of the first Christian university in Australia. This university would not have been possible without the help of the University of Notre Dame in the United States. As one chronicler of the history of this Australian institution wrote, "Indeed, the early Notre Dame (US) commitment and involvement was the perhaps most important single factor in causing this project to proceed beyond the feasibility study stage."[17] Protestants, interestingly, have not been able to imitate this model and not one broad Protestant university exists in Australia today. The need for the continual creation of Christian universities around the world still exists, and the Christian university must contribute to meeting it.

The Christian university has throughout history provided wisdom for a global church to help with complex forms of discipleship. Once the church grows in an area, it often builds universities to help with this task. Today, since global links are much easier to establish, we can now learn from the global Christian university in a whole new way about what it means to be the body of Christ and to live enriched lives of love for our global neighbors and our global God.

I was reminded of this reality when visiting a small Christian university in another country. Worship, as I have argued, shapes the heart of the Christian community since it nurtures and forms our love for God and neighbor. This Christian university, whose president says his one major priority is always to attend worship, sought to embody the creative and redemptive nature of God's kingdom in its worship service in a remarkable way. Once a month it invites members of the local L'Arche community, whose members share various physical and mental disabilities, to come worship with them. The sermon is conducted in a way that is most conducive to them and one or two of the disabled students even participate in leading worship service. In this way, the worship life of the university is also turned into a classroom of God's love for all humanity, even the least of these. I could not help but be impressed by what we can learn from the global Christian university.

QUESTIONS FOR DISCUSSION

1. How will the rationales for global learning be different at secular and Christian universities?

2. In what ways does our understanding of God and God's story shape how a Christian university approaches global learning?

---

17. Peter Tannock, "The Founding of the University of Notre Dame Australia: A Brief History of Its Establishment and Formative Years," June 16, 2008 (http://www.nd.edu.au/university/history.shtml).

3. What sparked the creation of your own university? How does its story fit into the larger story of the development of Christian universities?

4. How does your university currently encourage interaction with the global community, both Christian and non-Christian? What are some creative ways it could expand that interaction?

5. In what ways have you sought to extend your global learning and love for your global neighbor?

The Marks of an Educated Person

From a Christian standpoint, motivating and giving direction to all else are what we call "spiritual virtues": an unreserved commitment to God and his purposes for us in this world, a confidence in the Gospel, and a self-giving devotion—these which the Apostle calls faith, hope and love.[1]

—ARTHUR F. HOLMES, *THE IDEA OF A CHRISTIAN COLLEGE*

PART OF THE CHALLENGE facing the Christian university involves how to define an educated Christian person. The marks of an educated Christian person go far beyond criteria such as GPA, standardized test scores, and even the ability to amass the magic total of credit hours needed to graduate. Previous generations of Christian scholars such as Arthur Holmes indicated that an individual's ability to integrate his or her faith commitments was the definitive mark. While an important and laudable goal, determining the marks of an educated Christian begins with the questions of who we are, what orders or directs our loves, and how we steward our time, talents, and bodies in light of those realities.

Given the importance of this task, perhaps the best way to identify an educated Christian person is with a story—a story about a person who would not likely refer to himself as a Christian scholar but who nonetheless embodies the ability to answer the questions we all need to ask ourselves.

---

1. Arthur Holmes, *The Idea of a Christian College* (Grand Rapids: Eerdmans, 1987) 102.

A narrative account of someone who grappled with all of these questions at the deepest level is perhaps a more powerful and more succinct way of introducing this difference.

In high school, Lee Strand was not what you would refer to as a model student. If not for basketball and his desire to stay eligible for the high school team, he may not have attended enough classes to graduate. With the grandeur of the NBA calling, Lee assumed a career playing in the NBA was in his future. Lee's less-than-impressive efforts to attend classes were only matched by his grades. While a good basketball player, Lee would now be among the first to admit that his dreams of playing in the NBA were slightly unrealistic. In addition, he would now be the first to admit that playing basketball was not his greatest passion in life. However, he needed to have the opportunity to participate in a set of educational practices that would propel him to come to terms with what might be more important to him than basketball.

Despite doing his best in high school to avoid tapping into his abilities off the court, several universities offered him scholarships to play basketball, one of them a Christian university in Southern California. In the end, he chose that Christian university and found it to be a choice that would change his life in immeasurable ways. On the court, he continued to be a success. However, a mission trip 250 miles south of the United States' border with Mexico is what made the initial difference in terms of how he viewed himself and his life. An education major because he thought coaching was in his future, Lee signed up for the trip because it fulfilled his cross-cultural requirement. Most of the work he did in Mexico initially was helping to rebuild a structure designed to meet the educational needs of the children at an orphanage. Hanging drywall and installing metal siding on the roof proved to be among the safest of tasks. In this case, physical safety was not what was at stake, but rather his emotional safety. If the students stopped too long, they might encounter stories of neglect and abuse that would compel them to rethink their assumptions about the world and how it worked.

Being tall, Lee did his best to stick to working on the roof. However, a young boy who sat under a nearby tree for most of the day with the same tattered book in his hand eventually caught Lee's attention. Scaling down the ladder, Lee wandered over to the boy and mustered up the courage to inquire about the book in the little Spanish he knew. The little boy, Pedro, responded by telling Lee that the book, a book about fish, was his only possession that was truly his own and the only possession given to him by his mother before she died. Lee later learned that Pedro's father was in prison and that he had no contact with him. Lee asked if Pedro could read the book to him but Pedro said no because he only knew how to look at the pictures. Lee then asked if he could read the book to him. With eyes wide open and a smile stretching across his face, Pedro said yes. After reading it once, Pedro asked Lee to read it again, and again, and again, and again until the bell rang for dinner.

Giving Lee a big hug, Pedro then tried to give Lee his only possession in life as a thank you. Looking into the boy's eyes now with tears streaking down across his dusty cheeks, Lee wondered if it was rude to decline. In the end, though, Lee could not bring himself to take the book. Instead, Lee ran over to the supplies he and his fellow students had brought with them and found the books they had brought to donate to the orphanage's library. Finding a book on whales, Lee found Pedro in the dining hall and indicated he wanted to give it to him. Pedro eagerly accepted the book but wanted to make sure he and Lee made an even trade, thus once again trying to give him the book on fish. This time Lee obliged, thanked Pedro, and gave him a hug.

Unable to sleep that night, Lee wondered who he was as a person, why he got down from that ladder, why he went over to talk with Pedro, and how such an encounter would change his views on life once he crossed the border and headed home. In the end, Lee's introduction to the Christian story through his experiences in class, in chapel, and in the residence hall had left him with the understanding that all people were created in God's image—he and Pedro alike. If that was the case, why did he take so lightly the opportunity he had to attend classes and to read almost any book he might like? From that point on, Lee's life would never be the same. He did not have all of the answers. However, he was learning to ask the kinds of questions definitive of an educated Christian person.

Over a decade and a half later, Lee is now the regional superintendent of what is known as the improvement zone for one of the largest school districts in the United States. Four years after he graduated from college, he had won teacher of the year for not only his school district but also his county. His superintendent then asked him to work as his chief of staff. Lee said yes but only until the position of regional superintendent for the improvement zone became available. In that district of over 130,000 children, the improvement zone includes all of the schools not meeting minimal state standards. While Lee now has several honors to his credit that decorate his office, including the diploma he received when he earned his doctorate, his most prized possession and the one displayed most prominently is a tattered book on fish.

When asked by one reporter why the book on fish sat on his desk, Lee offered that the book was given to him by a little boy in an orphanage in Mexico. Prior to that moment in time, Lee indicated he was not a committed student. He failed to truly understand himself, how he spent his time, with whom he spent that time, and what his passions were in life. After that moment, Lee believed God had put a question in his heart that helped him answer all of these other questions. In essence, he believed God was asking him, "How do you now understand the value of your life when one of my children is willing to give you his only possession in his life?" Lee then explained to the reporter that each of the children in his district is a Pedro because each one of them was created in God's image. Needless to say, the NBA could not offer Lee such riches. Lee had become an educated Christian lover.

The purpose of the Christian university, we have argued, is to draw a particular community into the stories, settings, virtues, teachers, and practices designed to form within us a life given over to the complicated love of God and neighbor. As a result, the Christian university is called to be a place that cultivates a different vision of the educated person who seeks complex forms of wisdom and imaginative inspiration about how to love.

Today, however, the idea that professors should form lovers with wisdom is passé. Whereas past universities would be described as "factories for wisdom," contemporary universities consider themselves sources of technical expertise for professional practices. If their professors dispense advice beyond their discipline, it usually concerns matters of public policy or political life.

Consequently, professors operate with a narrow conception of their vocation. As one professor admitted, "There are many of my colleagues who would say, 'Look, we are at a university, and what I do is math; what I do is history. Moving into [moral or spiritual development] is not my competence.'"[2] To date, we have not found one secular university mission statement that claims to provide students with love or wisdom.

In contrast, Christian university faculty can mentor students and help them understand what loving God looks like when engaged in a particular

2. Alexander W. Astin, Helen S. Astin, and Jennifer A. Lindholm, *Cultivating the Spirit: How College Can Enhance Students' Inner Lives* (San Francisco: Jossey-Bass, 2011) 141.

vocation. For example, Christian educators should be able to provide students with wisdom about how to conduct research, to interact with sources, charitably interpret opposing views, and truly love their subject. They can remind Christian students that their vocation entails not merely studying and acquiring professional abilities, but first and foremost, acquiring the practices and virtues necessary for loving God and neighbors like Pedro.

In other words, they realize that the educated person needs to add a second conversation concerning the love of learning. Instead of being forced to learn, they learn for love. They then go on to embrace the complex process of becoming a creative and redemptive learner to fulfill that love. They seek to have their love "abound more and more in knowledge and depth of insight so that you may be able to discern what is best" (Phil 1:9b-10a). They habitually follow the rules of learning for its good, they continually practice a wide range of virtues in the process, and seek teachers to guide them in their various practices in all areas of life (and not just their vocation). They seek learning through wise teachers and models who can guide their practice and inspire creative faithfulness.

We should note that while Lee's story focused on his occupational vocation, the educated lover engages in this pursuit of wisdom for love in every area of life. Consider Habib Malik's testimony about his father, Charles Malik, a Lebanese philosopher and diplomat who worked with Eleanor Roosevelt to draft the United Nations Universal Declaration of Human Rights: "People ask me, what was it like growing up the son of a great man? My answer is, it was great! But only so because Charles Malik never let greatness detract from fatherhood."[3] We should, as Malik does, redefine the successful educated lover, to consider all of his or her roles and identities.

With great sophistication, Christian professors should also reflect on and communicate what it means to be good in such non-work vocations as being a friend, neighbor, citizen, son or daughter, future spouse, parent, or being a steward of creation, culture, and money. In reality, evangelicals are not the leading scholars, the sources of wisdom, in areas such as marriage, friendship, and fatherhood. While we may be known for political and cultural advocacy in these fields, we are much weaker at the present time when it comes to using academic disciplines to strengthen our wisdom about how to love in all areas of life.

---

3. Habib C. Malik, "Forward," in *The Two Tasks of the Christian Scholar*, edited by William Laine Craig and Paul M. Gould (Wheaton, IL: Crossway, 2007) 14.

To reach this end, Christian universities must hire faculty and staff who demonstrate the thinking, heart, virtues, and practices related to a well-lived Christian life, and the willingness to commend these things to others. Perhaps even more demanding, the Christian university will need to demonstrate God's grace and forgiveness when individuals or the whole academic community falls short of this ideal. Historically speaking, many of them have chosen instead to ignore this difficult challenge and focus on hiring primarily for academic expertise that focuses on technical knowledge.

In contrast, Christian faculty, administrators, and staff members should be able to articulate what it means to place Christ and their Christian identity first in life. Students, who are learning to prioritize and combine their own multiple identities and loyalties, surely profit from such wise counsel. Professors can constantly remind them that they are more than just students. Their grades do not constitute their worth and identity. They are first and foremost persons made in the image of God and redeemed by Christ.

Yet students need more than occasional admonitions. To approach this subject in a more complex fashion, professors could actually end their classes with a lecture about how their subject fits into their lives and how they put their lives together. We find that in general, students are most intrigued about how are we making decisions in the other areas of our lives: How do we balance being a professor with being a husband, father, citizen, and church member? How do we school our children in light of our education? How do we integrate not only faith and learning, but also faith, learning, and living? Students are interested in acquiring wisdom relevant to their loves. They long for the institution as a whole to witness to Christ in every dimension.

Of course, professors and administrators are not always wise and loving people. They have been socialized to be experts, not sources of wisdom and lovers. We hope they are wise enough to require students to read biographies of how people in their field and Christian saints in general have seen their lives redeemed under the power of the Holy Spirit. For example, we find that books related to issues about someone's life journey, like Augustine's *Confessions*, continuously fascinate our students. As Richard Foster writes, "In every age, great Christian saints have cultivated their life with God using the writings of Scripture, the theological reflections of others, the capacities of human reason, the cultural resources of the day and the spiritual disciplines. Through their reflections, the great saints witness to the work of the Holy Spirit and, when we study them, guide our spiritual life as well."[4]

Thus, since professors will always be deficient in this area when compared to great sources of wisdom and love, they should also point students to other mentors. They must continue, as Hebrews 11 reminds us, to help students contemplate the wisdom offered from the saints, those ultimate models of faithful love, in the Christian tradition.

If Christian universities hope to remain more than training grounds for narrow forms of competence, they must avoid the secular temptation to be satisfied with simply providing disciplinary expertise in a field of study. Such an education would not have proven to be enough in terms of Lee's interaction with Pedro. As a result, Christian universities must continue the grand quest to offer the world wisdom about what God's story of creation, fall, and redemption entails for the good life and a good world. That form of an education is worthy of efforts being made in both the Mexican desert and right next door to where we currently live. This side of eternity, we may never have all the answers. However, we will know the questions we should ask and trust in the wisdom God offers us to live faithfully in the meantime.

QUESTIONS FOR DISCUSSION:

1. In what way(s) if any, is your education preparing you to serve the needs of a young man like Pedro? If Pedro was right in front of you, is your education preparing you to truly see him as God would see him? If so, how?

2. How has the university cut itself off from the commitment to cultivate wisdom? In what ways, if any, are such threats present on your own campus? What can you do to help foster an environment where wisdom is cultivated?

3. What roles should professors play in the cultivation of wisdom? Administrators? Staff member? Students?

---

4. Richard J. Foster and Gayle D. Beebe, *Longing for God: Seven Paths of Christian Devotion* (Downers Grove, IL: InterVarsity, 2009) 15.

Suggestions for Further Reading

Budde, Michael L., and John Wright, eds. *Conflicting Allegiances: The Church-Based University in a Liberal Democratic Society*. Grand Rapids: Brazos, 2004.

Crisp, Oliver, Mervyn Davies, Gavin D'Costa, and Peter Hampson, eds. *Theology and Philosophy: Faith and Reason*. New York: Continuum, 2012.

D'Costa, Gavin. *Theology in the Public Square: Church, Academy, and Nation*. Malden, MA: Blackwell, 2005.

Ford, David F. *Christian Wisdom: Desiring and Learning in Love*. New York: Cambridge University Press, 2007.

Hampson, Peter, Gavin D'Costa, Mervyn Davies, and Oliver D. Crisp, eds. *Christianity and the Disciplines: The Transformation of the University*. New York: Continuum, 2012.

Hauerwas, Stanley. *The State of the University: Academic Knowledges and the Knowledge of God*. Malden, MA: Blackwell, 2007.

Higton, Mike. *A Theology of Higher Education*. New York: Oxford University Press, 2012.

Hughes, Richard T., and William B. Adrian. *Models for Christian Higher Education: Strategies for Success in the Twenty-First Century*. Grand Rapids: Eerdmans, 1997.

MacIntyre, Alasdair. *God, Philosophy, Universities: A Selective History of the Catholic Philosophical Tradition*. Lanham, MD: Rowman and Littlefield, 2009.

Marsden, George. *The Outrageous Idea of Christian Scholarship*. New York: Oxford University Press, 1997.

Smith, Christian. *What Is a Person? Rethinking Humanity, Social Life and the Moral Good from the Person Up*. Chicago: University of Chicago Press, 2010.

Smith, James K. A. *Desiring the Kingdom: Worship, Worldview, and Cultural Formation*. Grand Rapids: Baker Academic, 2009.

Smith, James K. A. *Imagining the Kingdom: How Worship Works*. Grand Rapids: Baker Academic, 2013.

Biblical Passage Index

Name and Subject Index

Name and Subject Index*

University of Notre Dame, 29, 31,
  84, 86, 140–41
University of Notre Dame Austra-
  lia, 140–41
University of Oxford, 9, 12
University of Paris, 9
University of San Marcos, 133
University of Virginia, 124

Valparaiso University, 63
Vanderbilt University, 88
visually impaired, 117–21
vocation, 68–80

Wenham, John, 12
Wesleyan (see Arminian)
Wheaton College, xiii, xvi, 124

William and Mary (see College of
  William and Mary)
William of Champeaux, 110
Wolfe, Tom, 96–97
women's rights, 109
worldview, 4, 49
worship, xiv-xv, 8, 14–25, 83, 98,
  101, 126–27, 139, 141
Wright, N. T. 12
Wuthnow, Robert, 68–69

Yale University, 9, 86
Yoder, John Howard, 86
Yong, Amos, 123, 127

zoology, 16

Made in the USA
San Bernardino, CA
01 July 2017